RYAN WINTERS

STOP OVERTHINKING

Daily habits for eliminate negative thoughts. How to make better decisions and master your emotions for start living with successful mindset

No part of this book may be reproduced or transmitted in any form or by any means, electronic or mechanical, including photocopying, recording or by any information storage and retrieval system, without written permission from the author, except for the inclusion of brief quotations in a review.

Limit of Liability and Disclaimer of Warranty: The publisher has used its best efforts in preparing this book, and the information provided herein is provided "as is." This book is designed to provide information and motivation to our readers. It is sold with the understanding that the publisher is not engaged to render any type of psychological, legal, or any other kind of professional advice. The content of each article is the sole expression and opinion of its author, and not necessarily that of the publisher. No warranties or guarantees are expressed or implied by the publisher's choice to include any of the content in this volume. Neither the publisher nor the individual author(s) shall be liable for any physical, psychological, emotional, financial, or commercial damages, including, but not limited to, special, incidental, consequential or other damages. Our views and rights are the same: You are responsible for your own choices, actions, and results.

Copyright © 2022 by Ryan Winters. All rights reserved.

DESCRIPTION 4

INTRODUCTION 7

CHAPTER 1 WHAT IS OVERTHINKING? 9

CHAPTER 2 WHAT CAUSES OVERTHINKING? 15

CHAPTER 3 ANXIETY AND OVERTHINKING 29

CHAPTER 4 HOW TO IDENTIFY IF YOU ARE AN OVERTHINKER 34

CHAPTER 5 INFORMATION OVERLOAD 47

CHAPTER 6 UNDERSTANDING POSITIVE AND DELIBERATE THINKING 65

CHAPTER 7 REMOVE NEGATIVE INFLUENCES 82

CHAPTER 8 STRATEGIES FOR ENDING OVERTHINKING 87

CHAPTER 9 THE MAGIC OF MINDFULNESS 104

CHAPTER 10 PRACTICING MINDFULNESS 118

CONCLUSION 136

Description

How many times in the past have you heard a coworker, a boss, or a loved one say the words, "stop overthinking it"? Maybe the question has been directed at you in the past, and you've responded with something like, "I'm not sure what you mean," or "I don't know if you're thinking through it *enough*."

Many times, communication is one of the main factors in the misunderstandings that occur between people in relationships. We say one thing, but it is understood in a different way. This complication is made worse when we fall into the habit of overthinking, which is simply taking in and processing way more information than is necessary to complete a given task or figure out a problem. When we pull from a much larger pool of information than is necessary for what we are trying to do, whether it's something as simple as picking out the appropriate tie or deciding whether to break up with that new boyfriend, we are guilty of overthinking and often make the task much harder on ourselves than it needs to be.

All those thoughts swirling around in your brain make even the simplest tasks difficult because it becomes nearly impossible to avoid distraction. Overthinking can lead to an emotionally damaging mindset, where you begin to think negatively about yourself, your loved ones, or even about the world.

Too much negativity and worry in your mind will shut out any hope of positive thinking or finding the path toward becoming a more positive, productive person.

I am excited to take this journey with you, and I know that you are about to discover many things about yourself as a person. The simple fact that you've sought out help from this book is an important first step forward. Many people continue through their entire lives living with the chaos going on inside their minds while they try to seek out a pleasant existence. But we're going much further than this. We're going to shed that old chaotic mindset and find the path to clarity.

This guide will focus on the following:
- What is overthinking?
- What causes overthinking?
- Anxiety and overthinking.
- How to identify if you are an overthinker
- Information overload
- Understanding positive and deliberate thinking
- Remove negative influences
- Strategies for ending overthinking
- The magic of mindfulness
- Practicing mindfulness... AND MORE!!!

Compartmentalization is an avoidance of the problem, and though it can be helpful in traumatic experiences, it is essential to address what is going on in our minds if we are to move past it. So, if you're ready, let's get started!

Introduction

As the name implies, overthinking simply means thinking too much. In reality, when you spend more time thinking instead of acting and engaging in other activities, then you're overthinking. You can find yourself analyzing, commenting, and repeating the same thoughts over and over again, rather than taking action, then you're overthinking. Such bad habits can hinder your progress, leaving one unproductive.

Each individual will experience overthinking differently and no two people overthink the same way. But generally, all those who overthink will agree that the quality of their life has been affected by their inability to control their negative thoughts and emotions. Such habits make it very difficult for the majority of the individuals to socialize, be productive at work, or enjoy hobbies due to the enormous amount of time and energy their mind consumes on a specific line of thoughts. Such uncontrolled emotions can be very harmful to the individual's mental health.

Overthinking makes it more difficult to make new friends and to keep friends; you will find it difficult to converse with them because you're overly concerned about what to say or what to do to keep the conversation going. Some individuals who are affected by this disorder may find it challenging to participate in general conversations or to interact with others even in a normal environment.

In addition, some may have trouble keeping an appointment or going to the store. This kind of thinking wastes time and drains your energy, thereby preventing you from taking action or exploring new ideas. It also hinders progress in life. This can be compared to attaching a chain that is connected to a pole around your waist and then running in circles you will be busy but not productive. Overthinking will disable your capacity to make sound decisions.

Under such circumstances, you're more likely to be worried, anxious, and devoid of inner peace of mind. However, when you stop overthinking, you will become more productive, happy, and will enjoy more peace.

Chapter 1 What is Overthinking?

Why Do We Overthink?

So far, there are two major explanations for the reason people overthink:

- The overthinking brain and
- Contemporary culture.

The Overthinking Brain

Our brain is designed in such a way that all our thoughts are interconnected in networks and nodes. For instance, thoughts about work may be in one network, and thoughts about family in another.

There is a strong connection between our emotions and moods. Activities or circumstances that stimulate negative feelings seem to be connected to one network, while those that induce happiness are linked to another network.

Although such interconnectedness of feeling and thought can help people to think more efficiently, it can also make people overthink.

In general, negative moods often activate negative thoughts and memories, even if such thoughts are unrelated.

Overthinking while in a negative mood can fill the mind

with lots of negative ideas and the more such a person overthinks, the easier it will be for his brain to induce negative associations.

According to research by brain experts, it has been discovered that damage (or miswiring) of certain areas of the brain can make one prone to depression and overthinking. Such areas include the amygdala and hippocampus, which are involved in learning and remembering, and the prefrontal cortex, which helps to regulate emotions. This knowledge partly explains why some individuals overthink more than others.

The Overthinking Generation. The reports from the studies conducted by the author showed that young ones, as well as middle-aged individuals, do overthink even more than the elderly ones (those above 65 years) do.

What can be responsible for this? There are 4 possible cultural trends that can be responsible:

- ***Entitlement obsession:*** Many today have an overdeveloped sense of entitlement. They are entitled to be rich, successful, and happy and as such, no one can hinder them from getting what they deserve. Thus, most people worry because they aren't getting what they deserve, they try to find out what is holding them back.

Such overthinking attitude has turned many into a ticking bomb, ready to explode at the slightest provocation.

- **The vacuum of values:** Majority of people today, especially the youth, have questioned all the values their parents handed over to them such as religion, culture, and social norms. Therefore, such ones are left with only a few choices and without values, such a person will end up questioning each choice he makes and keep wondering if he made the right choice. (This too can lead overthinking).

- **Belly button culture:** Modern culture and popular psychology often encourage people to be more expressive and to develop more self-awareness. However, most people often take this to the extreme, thereby becoming excessively self-absorbed, they overanalyze themselves and their feelings. Many people waste too much time "staring at their navels," brainstorming over the meaning of each emotional change.

- **The compulsive need for quick fixes:** The 21st century is filled with people who tend to search for quick fixes, instead of taking time to gradually work things out. For instance, if someone is sad or troubled, he can resort to some quick way out such as drinking alcohol, shopping, taking prescription drugs, engaging in a new sport or hobby, or some other activities. In summary, quick fixes only provide a temporary solution (or even wrong solution).

Overthinking Symptoms

Having a well-defined list of overthinking symptoms can be quite helpful. In fact, awareness is your best defense, it will help you to know when you are in the danger zone, and failure to be on guard is very dangerous for your mental well-being.

Watching out for the following symptoms can help you carry out an overthinking disorder test. If you observe that you are experiencing the overthinking disorder, you may observe one or more of these following symptoms:

- ***When you can't sleep:*** Try as hard as you may to get a decent rest, but your mind won't just turn off. Then agitation and worries set in.

- ***If you self-medicate:*** Research on overthinking disorder has shown that those suffering from it often resort to food, alcohol, drugs, or any means of modulating feelings.

- ***You're usually tired:*** Tiredness can be as a result of insomnia, or due to repeated thinking which drains the strength out of you.

- ***You want to be in control everything:*** You attempt to plan all aspects of your life to the very last detail. But the truth is, there's a limit to what you can control.

- ***You obsess about failure:*** The fear of failure has made you turn into a perfectionist and you often imagine how bad things will turn out if things don't work out well.

- ***You fear the future*:** Rather than being thrilled by what the future holds, you're stuck in your thoughts.

- ***You doubt your own judgment:*** You reconsider every decision you make from what you wear, to what you say, and how you relate with others.

- ***You get tension headaches:*** You might experience chronic tension headaches as though a tight band is around your temples. In addition, you might also feel pain or stiffness around the neck region. All these are signs that you need a long rest.

If any of the above signs happen all too often, psychologists will say you're an over-thinker or a ruminator. According to psychologists, over-thinking can affect performance, cause anxiety, or even lead to depression.

Chapter 2 What Causes Overthinking?

There are many, many causes of overthinking, many catalysts that trigger the bad habits of overthinking which can lead to anxiety and excessive worrying. These are not pleasant emotions, and what can seem like simply being careful and thinking things through can easily turn into something much more serious and damaging.

We've all experienced worry at some point in our lives. I remember when I was a child, my mother would leave the house very early in the morning to go to work at the post office, and I would wake up just as she was walking out the door and feel a desperate need to run out to the front door and catch her so I could say goodbye and "I love you." This didn't last long, but I remember for a few nights I was overcome by the worry that she was going to leave the house and I would never see her again. This is easily attributable to me being a young child but let us think about another example.

You are an adult, and your older brother is flying out to Colorado for a ski trip with his friends. He's just turned 21, and you know that there is going to be a good deal of partying and drinking going on. Now you start worrying about all the things that could happen. What if he gets in an accident driving around an unfamiliar area?

Would he be tempted to drink and drive? What if he falls while skiing and breaks a leg or an arm? What if he runs into a tree and has a concussion and he go to a hospital and I don't know about it because he doesn't have his phone and...and...and...

Okay, so this is an extreme case of acute worry, but I'm sure you know what I'm talking about and have experienced something similar concerning a loved one. To throw a wrench in the works, let's say you just watched a video on Facebook where someone ran right into a tree while skiing a few days ago. Now you have this mental image to feed those worries running through your mind like a broken record. Perhaps you saw a story about a car accident in Colorado caused by bad weather, and now you have that worry going through your mind.

An occasional bout of worry is perfectly normal, but when a person's life becomes plagued by constant worry about things that could happen without a good reason or basis, that person may be suffering from anxiety. There are different forms of anxiety, but two of the most common forms are social and generalized.

We may think of anxiety as a chronic form of overthinking, and many people experience such intense anxiety that they choose to take medication to assuage this feeling. Generalized anxiety applies to everyday experiences which most people get through without trouble.

Some people describe the feeling as a "fear of everything." Generalized anxiety affects day-to-day life and manifests as intense worry and fear of things like leaving the house, going to the grocery store, your loved ones' health, what will happen in the world, possibility of war, whether you are eating right, whether you might be sick with serious disease and not know it. Some people suffer from a specific phobia, but generalized anxiety tends to react to many different things at once and can become overwhelming.

You may have experienced some form of anxiety while you began to recognize the habit of overthinking. The first step to address overthinking is to figure out the causes that are specific to you. There are many causes to explore and you will learn as we discuss several of them, even if they don't all apply to you. Hopefully, as you read through this list, you will be able to pinpoint which factors may be playing the biggest role in your overthinking.

Social Expectation

Living and working in the world today is more demanding and challenging than ever before. Yes, we have the modern conveniences that make life more comfortable and convenient, but we also must contend with the structure of social life and the expectation that we follow a timeline that follows something like this: school, more school, entry-level career, climb the ladder, senior-level career, retirement.

For a long time, this was the norm for people living in countries of economic power. But a lot has been shifting over the course of the last few decades, and at an exponentially increasing rate. Finding a job in a lucrative career that will be enjoyable and satisfying for thirty or more years is not so simple anymore. The competition has grown right alongside the earth's population and the staggering advancement of technology. Many of the jobs readily available to our parents no longer exist, and nowadays, you would get a strange look for physically walking into a business and asking for an employment application instead of applying online. If you do manage to get that dream job right out of high school or college, then the real trial by fire begins. We could talk office politics, competition, and rivalry all day, but for right now, let's focus on some of the core triggers for overthinking in two of life's most influential domains: work and school.

We've started to discuss the challenge of finding gainful employment as a young adult in the modern age, so let's continue exploring where overthinking may come into play here.

Following the effect of globalization, the world is now overrun with advertisement and marketing schemes. From the very beginning of your career, you've been told that you will have to compete with many other candidates, many of whom may be more qualified than you. The interview process challenges candidates to make a compelling argument for why they should stand out above all the rest. You may practice in front of a mirror at home or think about all the possible questions that may come up. It is here when you may start thinking about how you measure up next to others in your field. You've just graduated from college with a degree and, at the time, you felt like you were on top of the world with a million different prospects awaiting you (best case scenario, of course). Fast forward a few months, and you start to realize that the job market is a tad more competitive than you thought, and you haven't proven yourself to be a shoo-in to some of your dream companies who have already passed on you. Many young adults in the millennial generation can attest to the challenges of having graduated during a recession in the US and having trouble finding any reasonable employment at all, let alone a prestigious start to a career in their fields.

The pressure of the social expectation that you can and will find a great job if you are smart and work hard enough becomes a great burden if and when things don't work out the way you'd imagined them throughout your time in school. At this point, you may begin to wonder if it is some fault or deficiency within yourself keeping you from your dreams.

The truth is, there are countless factors at play when it comes to finding or landing your "dream job," and sometimes, hard work and a positive attitude are just not enough, despite what your parents or teachers told you. This is why many young adults begin the cycle of overthinking that is dominated by questions of self-worth and adequacy. *If society says I'm supposed to be here or there at this point in my life, that means I've failed and there is something wrong with me.*

Once this conviction takes root, it is very hard to ignore the myriad images, slogans, and advertisements all around us which display the ideal professional man or woman in their nice corner offices, dressed in the latest fashions, sharing how they've made it this far because they work for this or that company, attended this or that school, bought this or that car, bought a house in this or that city, etc. This is when you may start to compare yourself to the success of others, which simply adds to the merry-go-round in your mind that feeds a feeling of inadequacy and low self-esteem.

But now let's say you've landed a decent job. It's not your dream job, but it may be a good start for you and your career. Now it's time to prove yourself. You immediately look around at your coworkers, boss, and peers to assess where you are on the ladder and how you measure up to your competition.

Depending on the type of personalities surrounding you, you may feel a lot of pressure to do well and grow within the company. Society teaches us that being the best is the only way to grow and climb within your company, so professional life instantly turns into a competition.

This pressure may manifest itself as overthinking every day as you constantly analyze how well you do your job.

This is not a bad thing in and of itself—everyone wants to be good at their jobs. A problem arises when we begin obsessively comparing ourselves to others, and when the job is no longer an environment of several likeminded people working to build a better company, but a cutthroat competition to the top.

Once you've managed to break into the top echelons of business society, the competition turns toward other companies in your field—overtaking their market, putting others out of business, etc. And we've all heard the saying, the more you gain, the more you have to lose. This opens up a whole new avenue of worry and overthinking as you assess how far you may fall if you make a mistake or fall off the ladder!

Is this you? Do you experience constant worry about where you are professionally? Maybe you are underemployed and feel embarrassed, like you haven't gone far enough in life as you compare yourself to others. This may be one of the most common triggers for overthinking, but now it's time to move backward in time to examine how social expectation first takes root in our minds as kids. Let's take a look at social expectation in school.

As kids, most of us aren't thinking seriously about what happens after school. We may have some far-fetched dreams swirling in our brains, but mostly we just want to know what mom packed for lunch today and if that big kid is going to knock us off the swing at recess again today. (Hopefully not, but you get the idea.)

As we grow older and enter the realms of middle school and high school, social pressure and expectation become more central to our lives in an immediate sense. We may be thinking of our future careers from a distance, but most of us are preoccupied with whether or not people like us at school, how popular we are, whether or not we'll get a date for the dance, etc. Much of the social pressure at this age centers around physical appearance and either academic or competitive achievement. Sadly, most girls around this age start to become overly concerned about their physical appearance and may even begin to equate this with their self-worth. The trigger for overthinking has begun as these women look around at the beautiful women in social media and in magazines, and begin comparing themselves to those unattainable ideals. Similarly, young boys may have a role model in sports or even a father figure who has become very successful in their professional fields and begin comparing themselves as men, equating success in competitive sports or popularity or academics with their self-worth.

The pressure only gets stronger as we enter college, if that is your path. Balancing social life with academic life is a struggle that many lose, resulting in a student dropping out of college.

Remaining focused and achieving good grades and that long-awaited bachelor's degree grants passage into the realm of professional work, where a whole new world of social pressure and expectation awaits.

As you can see, much of our overthinking may very well stem primarily from a distorted perception of ourselves in relationship to others in our professional or social environments. This pressure begins early in life and continues as we are constantly bombarded with images and messages in the media dictating what success should look and feel like.

Let's take a look at some more possible triggers for overthinking.

Relationships

Depending on your age, overthinking in romantic relationships can range from things like, "Does she like me?" to "I just know he's coming home late from work all the time because he's having an affair."

Much of the overthinking that occurs in the minds of people in relationships turns to emotionally painful sources of such feelings as jealousy and low self-esteem. Just as we are bombarded with images of "success" in the media, we are also bombarded with what it should look like to be in a perfect relationship. A young girl who obsesses over her looks in high school may later struggle in a relationship because she perceives other beautiful women as constant threats. Young boys who worry about making money may later struggle in a relationship because he thinks making money and working are more important than quality time spent with a partner.

Overthinking in relationships can cause a lot of problems, and many of them can be quite emotionally draining. When the thoughts taking over one's mind begin to cloud reality, you have the beginning of a self-destructive cycle of negative emotions and perceptions. Outside influences have a way of wheedling themselves into our minds and we begin comparing our relationships to those we see around us, on Facebook, or in other media sources.

This is a mistake because every person and relationship is

unique—there is no one-size-fits-all system for how a perfect relationship should work. You know you are overthinking when you get mad at your partner because he or she doesn't look at you the same way some famous celebrity looks at his or her partner. Comparing your romantic life to that of others is a great way to miss out on what makes yours special. I'm not saying you should ignore problems in your relationship. I'm saying you shouldn't try to compare those problems with others' problems as a way to solve them.

Each of us is unique, and we all deal with emotions and problems in different ways. Different doesn't mean wrong, but in a society that hides the challenges of a relationship behind the façade of a perfect one, people may experience quite the brutal slap in the face once they move past the "honeymoon phase," and begin to realize it's not all roses and stuffing cake in each other's faces. Relationships aren't supposed to be easy and breezy like the couple makes it seem on all those vacation resort commercials. Comparing and overthinking just makes the challenge more difficult—when the real necessity is communication.

Let's look at two more big sources of overthinking. The first is past trauma.

Trauma

Never a fun topic to broach, but a very important one if this is the cause of overthinking. As mentioned before, we've all experienced some degree of worry when it comes to the safety of ourselves or our loved ones. We worry about our children and their safety, about our spouses, and our aging parents' health, etc. The problem arises when these worries become an ever-present source of stress and anxiety—when the overthinking becomes chronic.

Many adults are affected for the rest of their lives after experiencing some kind of trauma. Many times, the death of a parent can lead to lifelong mindsets and perspectives that can hinder a person's openness and ability to move past painful emotions. Abuse as a child is a serious threat to a person's mental wellbeing and usually needs to be addressed throughout the person's life through treatments such as therapy. When a trauma occurs, it takes ahold of the mind in a way that is very difficult to forget or move past.

As a result, the individual may overthink in terms of comparing or viewing other events throughout her life through the lens of that trauma. For example, abuse of a child by an older male may distort a person's ability to deal with men in the future without feeling things like fear, hatred, or aggression.

These reactions encompass a much greater threat to overall wellbeing. Many adults manage to compartmentalize as we talked about earlier, or else completely forget or ignore the trauma until it crops up unexpectedly later in life.

This is an example of what we call "thought suppression." Sometimes, things are too painful to face, but many believe that the lifelong struggle to contain such pain will only lead to roadblocks in the progress of a person's life. In other words, eventually, the pain must be addressed.

On the level of overthinking, past trauma introduces thoughts and feelings about future events that have no bearing on the present. The fact that you were in a car accident and sustained horrific injuries as a teenager does not mean that every time you get in a car for the rest of your life, you're probably going to get in another accident, but it *feels* this way. We let the influence and strength of those past emotions and fears seep into the events of our lives, even before they've happened. Overthinking in anticipation of something bad happening is a trademark symptom of chronic overthinking.

Finally, I must mention arguably the most universal influence on overthinking—social media addiction.

Social Media

We are all familiar with the recent rhetoric surrounding how everyone is getting addicted to social media. Many of us can't go more than an hour without checking Facebook or our Twitter feeds to see what's new and who liked our latest posts, etc. What you may not realize is that addiction to social media is a powerful source of overthinking.

We've discussed such habits as comparing ourselves to others throughout our lives. One of the easiest ways to cultivate this habit is through social media.

When we look at a friend's Facebook page, odds are, we are seeing the pretty, superficially imposed perfect life that they want us and others on the internet to see. We see pictures of people that seem like they are off-the-cuff. But most people take a lot of time preparing their selfies, positioning themselves just right. Many women put on makeup then mess around with the filters until they present the most ideal versions of themselves, they can imagine. You don't see the challenges and stress in that person's life, you just see what they want you to see. This can lead to many of us, once again, comparing our lives to the lives of others who seem prettier, more successful, happier, richer, etc. Those negative feelings like jealousy and self-doubt creep up on us again, just like they did when we were younger and comparing ourselves to the prom queen or the football captain.

All of these thoughts build up over time, and eventually, they may take control, leading to a negative and self-destructive habit of overthinking.

Now that we've pinpointed some of the major triggers for overthinking, let's take a look at the phenomena that all that internet surfing and Facebook scrolling contribute to—information overload.

Chapter 3 Anxiety and Overthinking

Probably someone has once accused you of always creating problems for yourself out of insignificant issues. Personally, I think they are actually problems. How so? Simply put, anxiety makes you overthink anything and everything. Whenever we are anxious, we overthink things in various ways, and the product of our overthinking is not often beneficial. However, anxiety and overthinking should be temporary and should not be a permanent feature of our existence.

Ways anxiety causes overthinking

The end product of various types of anxiety is overthinking everything. There are various terms to describe how anxiety leads to overthinking. It is possible that this generic list will help you recall specific racing thoughts which you may have experienced or are likely experiencing and thus, help you realize that there are thousands of other individuals facing the same problem.

- Being overly concerned about who we are and how others view us or if we are measuring up to the world standard (this is a form of social and performance anxiety).
- Obsessing over what we should say/said/should have said/shouldn't say (another common social anxiety).

- Thinking about fearful possible scenarios such as: what if something bad should happen to us, our loved ones, or even the world (a common form of generalized anxiety disorder).

- Fearful, assumed results of our own wild thoughts, assumed faults, and feelings of incompetence (all forms of anxiety disorders).

- Anxiety over multiple obsessive thoughts, mostly scary ones, and thinking about them continually (a form of obsessive, compulsive disorder).

- Thinking, overthinking, vague thoughts, a tumbling chain of anxiety, and specific thoughts (all forms of anxiety disorders).

- Fear of experiencing panic attacks in public and feeling too scared to leave home due to such anxiety (a form of panic disorder with/without agoraphobia).

Result of anxiety and overthinking

When you're anxious, the thoughts do not just run through your brain and disappear, rather, they run through your brain continuously.

Those thoughts can be compared to an athlete running on a treadmill, he keeps running but gets nowhere in the end, left wired and tired.

One of the side effects of overthinking linked with anxiety is that we are likely to end up both physically and emotionally drained. Having bouts of the same anxious impulses run through our brain will definitely take its toll.

Another dark side of anxiety and overthinking is that sooner or later, we will begin to perceive everything that goes through our mind as reality. Perhaps we may believe that what we think about becomes reality and if we constantly think about it, it becomes very real. Right? No. This is one of the tricks anxieties tries to play on our minds.

But the good news is, we all have the capacity and the power to stop ourselves from being anxious and overthinking everything. Although, this is a process that involves multiple steps, at the moment, the best step you can take is to find something that can distract you from overthinking. Instead of battling with your thoughts, lowly divert your attention to something neutral, something else entirely. By pondering over something that is of no significance, you will be indirectly preventing overthinking everything.

The "leaven" effect

Overthinking has a "leaven effect" on your thoughts. Just like a dough, your mind can knead negative thoughts and, before you know it, it will rise to twice the initial size. F or instance, if a customer is dissatisfied with your services, you may begin to wonder if all the other customers are dissatisfied as well without giving it a second thought that probably most of the customers might actually be satisfied with your services. If care is not taken, with time, you might come to a discouraging conclusion that your services are not good enough. Your thoughts can even take you back to your marriage and you might begin to wonder if your mate is satisfied with you or if you're good enough for her or not. You think about how perfect she is, how she handles everything impressively, and conclude that you're totally unworthy of her.

The "distorted lens" effect

Another effect of overthinking is what is called the "distorted lens" effect and what this means, is that your thoughts only focus and magnify your faults or bad side and what your thoughts see is only hopelessness. For instance, when your kid comes home from school with a poor grade or gets into a fight, you may worry that he or she is growing up badly. Before long, you will start seeing yourself as a bad parent and that later in the future, your children will end up becoming bad adults.

What Overthinking Is Not

Worrying is quite different from overthinking. People often worry about things that can or may happen or possibly go wrong. Overthinkers; however, do more than just worry about the present, they also worry about the past and the future as well. While worriers think that bad things might happen; over thinkers think backward and they are very convinced that something bad had already happened.

Individuals with obsessive-compulsive disorder (OCD) are also different from overthinking. Those with OCD are overly obsessed about everything or every external factor, such as dirt or germs so they feel they have to wash their hands repeatedly to stay healthy. Such ones obsess about very specific actions and other matters that appear trivial or absurd to the rest of the world, such as "Did I lock the door?"

Chapter 4 How to Identify If You Are an Overthinker

The biggest cause of unhappiness is overthinking.

A big gap exists between deliberating and solving problems. Some often suggest that women are more likely to overthink than men, but the truth is that no one manages to avoid overthinking; it is something everyone does.

A therapist meets with thousands of individuals in their office daily, many of whom are searching for help in dealing with overthinking. Many often complain about their inability to relax. They feel that their brain is constantly preoccupied with worries and negative thoughts, and, as a result, they feel so much anxiety that they can't rest. Some complain about the fact that they focus excessively on how much better their lives would be without the mistakes they have made.

There is a strong connection between overthinking and mental health problems, such as anxiety and depression. Those suffering from overthinking might not even notice the decline in their mental health because they are so preoccupied and worried; they are not living in the mindfully. Such individuals might feel that their overthinking is healthy and useful, and without it some horrible calamity might happen.

But the truth is just the opposite. Overthinking increases the chances of feeling lost, anxious, and miserable. It can also lead to resentment and anger that clouds your judgment and makes it hard for you to make the right decisions. This state is often referred to as analysis paralysis.

Forms of Overthinking

Overthinking keeps reminding you of things you can't control, such as your failure. There are basically two forms of overthinking, namely: an excessive rumination on the past and worrying excessively about future events. These preoccupations prevent you from making progress in your life. There is a clear difference between overthinking, self-reflection, and problem-solving.

How is overthinking different from problem-solving? There is a clear difference between problem-solving and overthinking. When problem-solving, your goal is to solve an underlying problem. Overthinkers dwell more on the problems themselves than possible solutions to their problems.

How about self-reflection? Is it the same as overthinking? No! Self-reflection has a definite purpose; it helps you discover new things about yourself, your condition, and your situation.

What's the bottom line? While you are overthinking, you're not productive. However, self-reflection and problem-solving help you create solutions and recognize behaviors that may be holding you back.

Are You an Overthinker?

We all have a tendency to overthink. Being aware of this fact makes it easier to change. And the first step involves identifying the damage caused by overthinking.

The idea that overthinking stops bad things from happening is a subconscious perception nurtured by many; they feel that the failure to ruminate over past events will precipitate some sort of unforeseen calamity. Research indicates that overthinking is not healthy and will impact our lives negatively.

Ten Signs That You Are an Overthinker

Consider the following signs that show you're overthinking:

1. You repeatedly mentally revisit embarrassing moments in your head.
2. You find it difficult to sleep because your brain just won't shut off.
3. You ask yourself numerous questions, such as: What if?
4. You spend time thinking about the hidden meanings in events and social interactions.
5. You repeat past conversations you have had with others and think about things that you should or shouldn't have said.
6. You always remember your mistakes.
7. You keep playing a script of what someone did or said that you're angry about.
8. You lose track of current events happening around you because you're lost in deep thought about the future.
9. You spend time worrying about things you have little or no control over.
10. You can't rid your mind of your worries.

If you notice the tendency to become enmeshed in overthinking, don't despair. You can use the strategies below to get back your energy, time, and brainpower.

From proper time scheduling to thought substitution, here are several exercises that will boost your mental strength and help you stop overthinking everything.

Things Overthinkers Do (That They Never Talk About)

If you are an overthinker, you limit your chances of becoming successful in life. It will prevent you from reaching your goals and make your life miserable.

Below are ten of the things overthinkers do without paying attention to;

They apologize excessively

When you tell an overthinker that they have wronged you, before even identifying if the situation is their fault, they start to apologize. This leaves them exposed to additional criticism, which may or may not be warranted.

It is good to accept blame and reduce others' tension sometimes, but if this is done exclusively to please others, or because you're scared of what they will think about you, it is unhealthy.

An overthinker always wants to smooth things over with other people. This causes them more pain in the long run.

Critical thinking is their thing

Most overthinkers are excellent critical thinkers. This is one of the excellent things about overthinking. An overthinker spends all of their time deliberating and analyzing each decision in an unending manner. Therefore, they often come up with the best results.

Overthinkers can punch their way out of a paper bag, but only after analyzing the entire makeup of the bag, and the soft spots. That takes a whole lot of time, but they deliver the best results. Often, overthinkers use their tunnel vision to focus relentlessly on a problem until they come up with a solution.

Sleeping is an issue

An overthinker's brain never stops working. It keeps spinning at maximum speed all day long. This makes them restless, and sleeping becomes impossible. Their minds refuse to shut down, even when their body needs sleep.

They worry excessively about making others happy

Overthinkers forget that they should be happy too. They worry about others' happiness, forgetting they need to be happy. They often negatively exaggerate how the world will view their feelings, actions, thoughts, decisions, and words.

This limits their progress and makes accomplishing their personal goals harder. They make decisions that please others, instead of themselves.

Overthinkers May Also Be Escape Artists

In order to escape their own minds, overthinkers might resort to overworking, excessive activity, perfectionism, and other extreme habits to escape from their overthinking.

Those with more serious issues may turn to state-altering medications or drugs to take the edge off.

They experience severe headaches or migraines

Catastrophic overthinking may cause somatization, such as headaches, stomachaches, etc. Those especially prone to worrying or overthinking may fear that their headache is a symptom of something more serious, which may make their headache even worse.

They research their purchases excessively or always need a second opinion

When making purchases, those that overthink may become paralyzed with the overabundance of options that are available to them. They may search online for hours for the best options. They may ask all of their friends' opinions.

When shopping, they may need to consider multiple options or ask a friend to come along just to approve their choice. This comes from a place of low self-confidence. They wait for others to decide or approve what they will eat, wear, and do.

Their overthinking stems from insecurity

They often overthink because they are unsure of their decisions; this makes it hard for them to decide on what to do.

At work, they might have issues choosing clients, projects, or the best course of action to take when problems arise. This lack of confidence can lead them to be doubted by others, even when they end up making the right decisions.

They may become overly preoccupied

They may not be able to see the forest for the trees. When they become overly preoccupied, they may miss important dates or appointments.

They may search endlessly for reasons to stop overthinking

Some often admit that they overthink; it may be something that they always try to break free from. They may overthink about ways to stop overthinking.

19 Things You Need to Stop Overthinking

Specifically, while there are a lot of things that people overthink about, there are some aspects of life that a person shouldn't even waste his or her time thinking about.

Let's check them out one by one.

1. Whether You Love or You Don't Love Someone

That shouldn't be rocket science. Because, finally, you either do or do not. For sure, whether you love the person or not, you will eventually know.

2. If the One Who You Love is The One You Will Want Forever

There is no genuine or sincere timeline; the only timeline is the stereotype that society portrays today. When you don't follow it, it might make you feel ashamed. For a lifelong decision, you don't have to be sure right away; many people aren't sure right away, either.

3. Mundane Social Discrepancies

You fear that people do not want to talk with/to you; as a result, you worry or think they don't want to hang out with you. No, that isn't necessarily the case. Sometimes, people don't have the time. So, don't panic automatically. The only time it means something is when someone says to your face that they aren't into you.

4. How You Appear to Others

How people view you depends on the filter that they view you through. This includes their own biases and beliefs about others. What they think and feel about you will seem accurate to them, but it might not reflect the real you. Know yourself and be positive.

5. The Difference Between What Someone Says and What They Mean

People don't always mean what they say! It can sometimes

be easy for you to identify when they aren't entirely honest with you. Yes, it's a gut feeling; their body language speaks volumes. However, sometimes people will not be honest with you, and you will have to take them at their word, or not at all.

6. The Grand Scheme of Things

Have you ever thought about how grand the whole world is? At a point, do you feel like proceeding? Certainly not! The vastness and mightiness of the universe, on the other hand, is awe-inspiring, and spending time to understand the details is an interesting but unproductive use of our imaginations.

7. Your Exact Place in the World

Don't compare yourself to anyone. Where you are right now is your place. If you want to change, your subsequent destination is your new place. When it comes to where one needs to be in life, there is no right and wrong answer.

8. Whether You Are Happy or Not

When you are overthinking about whether you are happy or not, you are not satisfied. Do you feel you delighted? If answering that is tough, then you are not happy.

9. **Whether You Have Made a Bad Decision or Not**

   If you keep dwelling on past choices, you will not change anything in your future. The right thing to think about is the step that you should take next.

10. **Whether you should meet up with someone and hang out**

    You have many assumptions in your head: Will they say no, yes, or maybe? Will they reject you outright? Chances are they don't know what's in your mind. So, what's healthy here is give it a try. They might feel flattered and happy that you want to spend time with them and strengthen the relationship.

11. **Every minute detail about why some things didn't work out**

    The moment has passed! You will not get the chance to work these things out now. So, let them go! For the sake of growth, you could reflect on those occasions, so you don't make the same mistakes again. However, when you overthink them, you will bury yourself in sadness and remorse.

12. **How society will define you**

    Society's labels don't define you. They are simply what people use to identify you. You do not have to use them to identify yourself.

13. Jokes

Sadly, many people overthink an excellent joke and become upset. They should just try to enjoy it. Overthinking jokes saps your joy. So, don't worry about what's behind everything that some people say.

14. Higher spiritual and deeper philosophical meanings behind everything

Most times, we don't need to know. And you will never know for sure, unfortunately.

15. Writing an email

You should not re-read emails excessively before sending them. Imagine spending hours wondering if your email would make sense. Should you write it this way? I'm not saying one shouldn't think about this at all, but you should only spend a few moments composing and fine-tuning your message. So, while you need to be conscious of your words, don't overthink to the point that you will have to discard the idea of sending the mail entirely.

16. What your social media presence reveals about you

I'm impressed by people who do not usually post pictures of their success and achievements on social media. It tells me that they are out there, living their lives and enjoying them, and that they are not sidetracked with what goes on around them. Also, it shows they immersed in the process of achieving their goals.

17. How your old self would see you

At certain stages in life, we have moments where we sit and ask ourselves how our younger self would see us. We could think thoughts like: How would I, five years ago, feel about me right now? He would be so disappointed in me. Well, forget about the old you for now; you're past that for a reason. The current you made certain decisions for a reason as well; respect them and respect your current self.

18. Your output at work

You may not always get complimented for a job well done. Most times, you just have to do your best and let everything else fall into place. You won't get any better at what you do by trying to get every colleague's opinion about your activities; it will just drive you crazy.

19. Whether or Not to Talk to a Loved One

It's much quicker to simply just send a text or pick up the phone and call them.

Chapter 5 Information Overload

Overthinking can drain your sanity, mental and physical energy, and time.

The issue is, we are all accountable for it. We have been told to end overthinking.

There is a massive disparity between creative thinking and overthinking. If you think creatively, you are not looking to downsize a decision. Instead, you are making a whole new decision overall.

Creative thinking indeed is helpful. It helps in building new ideas which can result in a positive outcome.

However, overthinking is not healthy. It makes our ideas stagnant.

So, here is what must know about overthinking and how it can destroy conversions.

Cognitive Bias

How people think, plays a vital role in overthinking.

From the way you have raised, lived as well as worked, all of us developed a cognitive bias.

So, meaning as a human being, we are geared towards doing or thinking things in a specific manner, and most of the time which can cloud our judgment.

Above are some of the many examples of passive biases which can twist our thinking process. Many famous conversion killers we have discovered include information and confirmation bias.

Confirmation Bias

Confirmation bias creeps wherever and all over. Usually, we look for information which justifies our very own preconceptions; or instead, we screw up details to fall in line.

Confirmation bias kills conversion, as we aren't always right. Regardless of the experiences you had before. Almost every market usually is different six months later.

There is an idea, which development is just an exceptional one. Like for instance, Airbnb grew, do you believe you could copy that in any business? Certainly not!

Since we had been successful some time ago, it doesn't mean we can idle by and do the same thing time again and again. Instead of being open-minded, it is simpler to prove to others, that, "maybe it will work yet again."

Information Bias

Due to the development of the internet, information bias is now easy to develop.

People take a data-driven method to decisions. They read far too many blogs. Most of the time, those blogs are not even relevant to what you are trying to obtain.

Sometimes, forty to seventy percent of the information required in making a choice is just enough. Spending a lot of time looking to rationalize edge-case scenarios can delay your decision. What is more, you also waste valuable time mentally testing thought, rather than putting it into action.

There is a similarity between information bias and information overload; however, in information overload, the issue is not searching for the information, but how much you have assimilated.

Seeking a lot of resources, seeking a lot of data burns you out. And if you are already exhausted, you aren't taking action. Thus, you are overload.

Come to think of it, and you have just put as one a development technique you have decided to do a bit further examination. You keep on reading, then suddenly, you are beginning to think more about whether or not what you have put jointly works.

You are taking in lots of information, and instead of carting off the key pieces, you are getting caught. Your developments and frontward momentum disappear.

Sad to say, most of the time, doing a lot is our biggest conversion destroyer, rather than trying structuring goals and breaking the whole thing down into more convenient milestones.

According to Seth Godin, "The cost of being wrong, is less than the cost of doing nothing."

If you are in doubt, be interested and test. You are destroying your conversion by doing nothing. You also are killing your conversion as you are trapped in information overload. All of these are not doing you any good.

Physical and Mental Symptoms Which Point Toward Information Overload

The whole thing should be done in moderation, including the assimilation of knowledge. Or else, it can seriously affect your physical and mental well-being in so many ways such as:

- Increase your blood pressure
- Low energy or mood

A significant decreased in cognitive performance that ultimately affects the skills in making a choice

- Impaired vision
- Finding it hard to focus
- Strong pressure to check apps, voice mails, emails, etc
- Diminished productivity
- Vivid dreams
- Insomnia
- Tiredness

All these are symptoms that you are experiencing information overload.

What Should You Do to Keep Away from Information Overload?

Without a doubt, you are hungry and curious for information because accessing it anytime, and wherever is easy. No matter what idea comes into your mind, you want information about it and you check as a lot of resources as you can.

However, understanding the risks you expose yourself to, you must opt for solutions and techniques which will make sure a normal function of your brain.

Check the information

Just listen and read the information you think valuable for today. Choose information that can enhance your skills and knowledge. Or else, take for granted irrelevant information such as gossips, news, talk shows, and many others.

Choose Reliable Sources: It's always better to hear diverse opinions; however, more doesn't mean truer or better. Just pick the best sources.

Set a Limit

Is it really needed to read the news each morning or keep your posts updated daily on Twitter and Facebook? Set a time limit and avoid spending lots of time a day browsing social media sites or the news you read concerning your favorite Hollywood artist.

Prioritize Activities

There are some activities which are vital than others. Avoid overloading your schedule with lots of activities which need too much of your time and attention. Finish first the most vital one and if you have more time, do the next one.

Choose Conversations Smartly

A lot of people are able to leave you mentally or emotionally drained. Some might want to talk a lot and provide you lots of information as possible, while some will pass their concerns to you. Your energy and time are limited, therefore spend them smartly.

Learn How to Say No

If some projects are of your skill or knowledge, don't afraid or hesitate to say no. Additional work will decrease the quality and efficiency of your cognitive performance. In turn, this will not provide the outcomes you have been looking for.

Do What is Right

Yearly, there are a growing number of young people all over the world who died due to stroke. According to expert, one reason for this devastating fact is the overstimulation of their brain as they have a lot of responsibilities.

As a result, professionals recommend that you must re-energize your neuron and boost your resistance to damage by doing simple things like exercise, hydration, outdoor activities, and enough sleep.

Give More Time to Yourself

Spending time along can refresh your mind. So, take a break, and put all your thoughts and thinking into order by doing nothing, keep away from people, bad influences, and social media.

If you are experiencing the signs of information overload, what techniques do you apply to look for psychological balance?

Avoid Information Overload to End Overthinking!

The most actionable takeaways:

- Give more of your time on getting things completed, concentrate on the action. Spend lots of your time in making progress and spend less time in negative thinking.
- Break things down into easy to handle chunks
- Overthink less and test more
- Avoid reading too much, and do not look for too much information.
- Be aware of why you're here, who you are, and where you are.

Knowing the Setback of Overthinking

As an individual, it is vital to understand the setback of obsessive thinking. It is also vital to know how to keep away from it. Most of the time, when we get in our heads, we get into problem. A new study conducted in the U.K involving 30,000 individuals revealed that giving so much time on negative things or events (specifically through self-blame and rumination) can be the most important predictor of today's most popular mental health issues.

Conquer Your Critical Inner Voice co-author, Dr. Lisa Firestone commented, 'time spent in thinking and reflection is constructive and optimistic- a rich setting for creativity and personal development. However, entering in our mind can also be harmful once we are unconstructively turned in opposition to ourselves. She also commented that there is a significant disparity between rumination and introspection. According to Dr. Lisa Firestone, introspection takes account of self-examination and healthy self-reflection. But rumination is like a brutal cycle of unconstructive thinking. It is discouraging and critical self-talk. Introspection can result in insights, self-understanding, solution, and goal setting. Rumination, however, can lead to self-doubting, makes you feel critical and stifled. This is also self-destructive.

In obsessive thinking, we engage in an unhelpful thought process which results in hostile results.

We're listening to what Doctor Lisa refers to as a critical inner voice in our mind which sharpens in on the unconstructive factors of circumstances. This inner voice is like an aggressive coach, which feeds us a continuous flow of criticism and challenges and demoralizes our objectives. It is that thought which comes once we are about to go in various conditions like a job interview. You will fail this, and you are not capable of getting the position. Just like how worried you are. It is the conversation which plays in your mind evaluating your relationship: Why did she ignore more presence or why is she cold today? Perhaps I did or said something offending. She is losing interest. Perhaps she already finds someone else.

Therefore, why do people harbor this internal opponent which feed them awful advice and unconstructive commentary? The reality is that human beings are divided. We are divided between our anti-self and our real-self. Although our real-life is objective-directed, life-affirming as well as signifies our real desires and values, our anti-self is like an internal opponent that is self-critical, self, denying, doubtful and fearful, both towards us as well as towards others.

Keep in mind that real-self is developed from constructive experiences in life, healthy growth events, as well as traits and qualities we have seen in our loved ones and early caretakers.

Anti-shelf is formed from our unconstructive experiences, damaging attitudes, and harmful occurrences we were encountered during our early lives.

Like for instance, if you have a caretaker who sees you as no good, your inner voice tends to replicate this upsetting and cruel approach toward ourselves. As mature individuals, we are likely to self- parent, telling ourselves similar things we were told as kids. When you side with your anti-self and pay attention to your "critical inner voice," you can be led down a hurtful way which is not based on truth and reality. You might engage in an unhelpful flow of rumination, a kind of obsessive thinking which has been associated with stress, sadness as well as suicide.

It doesn't matter if you beat yourself up over a blunder you made in the past or worry about how you are going to succeed in the future, worrier is overwhelmed by anguishing thoughts- and their incapability to escape from you own head leaves you in a condition of continuous anguish.

While we think so much on a specific matter every now and then, some people cannot ever seem to settle down the continuous flows of thoughts. The inner monologue of these individuals takes account of two unhelpful and negative thought patterns- worrying and ruminating.

Screaming STOP or I Can't Take it Anymore Will Not Help You!

If you can stop yourself from overthinking things, screams STOP, shatter a rubber band, set off a shock, then you would not be here. Sad to say, there is no off switch for overthinking. Screaming STOP is indeed the most innate reaction to overthinking. However, experts have found out that the effort to hinder some thoughts from consciousness results in an opposite and equal reply wherein the thoughts you are trying to hold back come swinging back with a revenge. Telling yourself to end thinking so much is like pressing on a ball under the water. Once you press harder, it pops higher. Thus, you aren't able to hold onto it.

Obsessed thinking an event, problem, or a conversation is a common way of dealing with anxiety. On the other hand, researches conducted by experts reveal that obsessed thinking and pondering is something worrying and stressful. It has a strong connection with stress, sadness, and depression. For a lot of people out there, overthinking a specific matter is only a habitual way of viewing the world surrounds them. But, that state of mind can result in extended periods of sadness. Research also reveals that can lead to some people to setback seeking medication. Knowing to deal with this kind of condition can help a person to set free of painful and hurtful occurrences in life and break out of damaging thought patterns.

Learn the Various Cognitive Distortions

Prior to starting to solve or cope with this condition, first and foremost, you will have to know what types of thoughts take place when you are engaging in this harmful activity. Any time you find yourself pandering to these unpleasant, painful, and self-doubting thoughts, you're on the way to obsessed thinking due to the cognitive distortions. Similarly, if you find yourself giving reasons to no carry-out something, or making reason and justification for your self-doubt. Most popular cognitive distortions take account of the following:

All or nothing thoughts: you believe in things which are absolute and viewing each condition as being black or white.

Overgeneralization: viewing one unconstructive occurrence as a constant flow of embarrassment or defeat.

Mental filtering: just settling on unconstructive things which include results, feeling as well as thoughts, while taking for granted all the optimistic and helpful factors of those scenarios or situations.

Discounting the optimistic: believing that no one in your admirable features or achievements matter.

Jumping to conclusions: either supposing that others are thinking/ responding unconstructively towards you without any proof (this also known as mind-reading) or believing that an incident will be worse without any proof for this conclusion.

Emotional reasoning: this signifies believing that how you feel mirrors a truth about yourself.

Minimization or magnification: this refers to blowing unconstructive things out of proportion or minimizing the value of good deeds.

"Should" declarations: this refers to punishing yourself for things which should and should not be done and said.

Labeling: this refers to turning shortcomings or mistakes into a feature attribute of yourself. Like for instance, turning the idea "I was wrong" into "I am a failure, or I am a loser."

Blame and personalization: this refers to internalizing mistake for cases or occurrences you are not liable for or blaming someone for events and situations which they had no control over.

See How You Overthink

There are many avenues for a person to overthink everything; some of these are because of cognitive distortions. Catastrophizing is one kind of overthinking. This thought pattern takes place anytime you instantly foresee an unconstructive result in some occurrence or series of occurrences and jump to the conclusion that such a result would be unbearable or devastating. This thought pattern is a mixture of overgeneralizing things and jumping straight to the conclusion.

Trying to know the specific cognitive distortions that affect your overthinking is very important. Put down the thoughts you suffer, and try to categorize which ones could fall into the classification of cognitive distortions.

You need to practice learning to distinguish your overthinking thoughts as they come up. By simply labeling your thoughts once you become sensitive to them might help a lot. Try silently uttering the word "thinking" as you start to overthink, might help you in grounding as well as breaking out the increasing thought pattern.

Always Pay Close Attention to your Feeling

Falling into autopilot type during the period of your day is easy. On the other hand, once your time or day is filled with events which can encourage stress and depression, you might be walking blindly into an event which will lead you to think so much and catastrophize.

Try to Command A Personal "Check-In"

Evaluate how you are feeling as you come into different situations and scenario which are likely to induce the pattern of overthinking.

Determine any case in point in which you start to pander to patterns of thinking so much. You have to avoid judging yourself from it, appreciate it prior to working to alter it.

Challenge Automatic Thoughts

If you have recognized an event of catastrophizing or overthinking, now you can start to dispute the legality of those feelings and beliefs. Challenging the thoughts by means of remembering that feelings and beliefs aren't facts might help you escape from the pattern of overthinking.

Feelings and beliefs aren't always a sign of actuality and authenticity. Most of the time, these thoughts are uninformed, warped, or just wrong. By allowing setting a reliable insight of perception of beliefs free, you will be more able to consider other potentials. Or accept that overthinking is not always right.

Look at what real, objective proof you have to back the cognitive distortions and overthinking patterns which you are experiencing. There's a good possibility that you'll not be capable of coming up with real, compelling proof that the beliefs and feelings you are experiencing right now have any grounds inaccuracy.

Silently trying to say, "These are only thoughts, and these aren't real." Saying this mantra over and over again might help a lot in disengaging from the increasing thought patterns you are stuck in.

Substitute and Swap these Cognitive Distortions with Genuine Facts

Once the pattern of overthinking is increasingly becoming out of your control, you may feel it so hard to get away that thought pattern. On the other hand, if you know how to determine what thoughts you are experiencing right now are not real, then you can fairly and easily swap that pattern of thought with a more realistic and truthful one. Try to say this thing to yourself, "If I admit that my theories and overthinking aren't basis in facts, then what are the truths in this case?"

Although a condition ended defectively and imperfectly, you can give more of your time on what to carry out another way in the future as an option to dwelling on what you must have done or said in the past. At first, it will not easily come. On the other hand, if you retrain your mind to process events in another way, sooner or later everything will be easier for you.

Try to Ask Friends or Loved Ones Who Are Receptive to the Condition for their Participation or Input

At times asking a trusted colleague, relative or a friend whether you are overthinking or overreacting to everything can help in realizing that there is no reason for you to keep on thinking that way.

Positive Self-Talk Can Replace Overthinking and Self-Doubt

How you talk to yourself has an impact on your feeling. So, rather than criticizing yourself or pondering on bad feelings, try to spend your time on the things you excel.

Are you good at writing? Do you love singing and dancing?

Give more of your time to the things that make you happy. This will not just help you get away from ruminating bad things.

Chapter 6 Understanding Positive and Deliberate Thinking

In order for us to overcome the habits of overthinking, it is important that we first understand two of our biggest allies on this front: the power of positive thought and the power of deliberate thought. Both of these concepts play a very large part in the successful replacement of negative thoughts with thoughts that serve and benefit you. By understanding what positive and deliberate thinking is, and how your mind and body reacts to them, you are able to use these tools to slow the negative momentum you currently have and build momentum in a desirable direction instead.

Positive Thinking

It can represent different things to different people, but the best way to understand positive thinking is to think of it as an attitude. The individual who uses positive thinking carries this attitude and conducts their thoughts and actions according to it. It is the individual's goal to feel good as often as possible, and he or she uses any tool possible to accomplish it. This often means that when circumstances seem undesirable, it is the positive thinker who finds the positive aspect, but not because they are deluded about the truth. Simply because the priority to feel good is higher. The individual seeks to make the experience as pleasant as possible.

It is often the case that positive thinkers once were over thinkers. It is not uncommon for a healthy mind to think critically and practically, and to analyze circumstances and scenarios. However, sometimes that healthy critical-thinking turns to rumination or worry and the individual breaks off into a tangent about anything. The mind and body have learned the habit of analyzing every situation, no matter how significant, and even to over-analyze it. The mind and body have learned from previous experiences that analyzing, planning, and preparing creates the safest circumstances for you when there is a negative impact.

To guard against damage from negative impact, the mind and body continue to follow the pattern it has been taught; to overthink. However, at some point, the thought-pattern; the behavior, fails as a guard against the impacts of life and instead, only damage has been done to the individual through worry and obsession.

The individuals started as critical, analytical, thinkers and they continue to be. Many of these over thinkers recognize that they cannot continue to repeat the same thoughts and habits and achieve different results. For different results, there must be different thoughts and actions.

Even one of the most widely referenced scientists of our time, Albert Einstein, reminds us that scientifically, we cannot repeat the same actions and get different results.

Scientifically, philosophically, this is the case. Rather than fight this law, the critical thinker applies it, and changes from the old, negative thought patterns to the positive replacement thoughts that feel good to focus on and spin tangents around. By doing this, the critical thinker does not struggle with the mind's tendency to wander. Essentially meaning if you want to spin tangents and daydreams, spin them around ideas that feel good to think about.

Positive thinking is not just the practice of good-feeling thoughts and ideas; it is also very much the observation and recognition of the thought-patterns and behaviors you currently repeat now. It takes bravery to be a positive thinker; you cannot fudge the truth and lie to yourself so easily. You have to be brave enough to see yourself where you are in an objective way. When you can make this observation with an objective lens, it becomes much easier to excel at making these positive changes to your patterns of thought and behavior.

There is not just one way to practice positive thinking. There are many different ways to apply this practice to your life. You need not master them all; just find a few you like, that really feels good for you and use those. Add a new technique here and there for fun.

Without the practice of positive thinking, it can become a tricky pursuit to stop negative thoughts and behaviors.

Often what will happen without a positive pattern to replace a negative one is that one negative habit will be replaced with another negative and harmful behavior? For example, if an individual practices binge smoking to cope with anxiety, and he or she stops smoking, this might be replaced with binge-eating, or another negative behavior or thought-obsession where the smoking once was. This occurs because we tend to learn more negative coping skills than positive ones.

When you first begin positive thinking, it can feel as if you have no momentum going in that direction. That is okay. This path may not have been used much and it will take some treading to gain momentum. That is okay. The more you hone it, the more effortless it becomes.

Recognize Negative Thinking

One of the first steps in making a change to add more positive thinking to your routine is to recognize negative thinking when and where it happens. There are often times we can be harder on ourselves than others are and, in some cases, this can be caused by purely physiological reasons and have little to do with our emotions.

Consider times when you are exhausted from physical exertion or a time when you are sick with a cold or flu or even allergies. The physical stress that the body experiences while it tries to repair itself can cause you to focus on the other topics in your periphery that echo those feelings of exhaustion or sickness. This focus on the negative begets more negative thoughts and very often this can come in the form of self-criticism, especially if you're lying in bed sick with nothing much to do but ruminate in your own head and stew in your own thoughts. Ask yourself: is the stew full of nutrients or toxins.

The same can happen if you are experiencing trouble sleeping or if you have not eaten well or at all. The phrase "hangry" is a recent representation of this occurrence made known by Snickers ads.

Hangry, of course, is a combination word made from "hungry" and "angry" and meaning that if one does not eat; he or she will become moody and angry with others until sustenance has been eaten.

In the same way, that being overtired or hungry can make you angry, it can also play a role in how much negative thought and behavior you resort to, out of habit and as a coping mechanism.

Though some negative thinking comes because of physical sickness and exhaustion, much negative thinking is the result of the mental and emotional stress of some kind. This stress could be expressed as any number of mental or emotional disorders such as PTSD or clinical depression. In some cases, there is actually a physiological response triggering in the individual that may put them into a period of deeper anxiety or depression, and for this reason, it could be said that is yet another physical cause of negative thinking, though the physical mechanism occurs in the nervous system. During these periods, an individual may practice heightened self-criticism and negative thought.

Similar circumstances arise when an individual is put into a situation of high stress or pressure, or when there is a high level of obligation or expectation from the individual. These circumstances can easily trigger an individual to think and act in a more negative and self-critical way. The body and mind react this way out of habit to plan and protect the individual. Nevertheless, as we have seen, this negative behavior is mistaken for a healthy beneficial process simply because the mind thinks it helps to guard against impact from the world.

Regardless of what triggers the individual for negative thinking, like attracts like and soon the individual is drowning in only thoughts that represent negativity, doubt, and worry. It works very much like a train on the tracks. Let us say your train is pulling out of the station. It is heading in one direction and slowly picks up speed. Slow at first and the wheels start pumping, but soon the train is headed in one direction with great momentum. Thinking gains momentum in the same way. When you start to build momentum in the direction of negative thoughts and ideas, the more you repeat and dwell in those negative ideas, the faster your momentum builds in that direction. But good news: positive thinking can build the same powerful momentum.

When the train is moving in one direction with great momentum that is a bad time to step in front of it or pull the emergency brake. Braking fast and bringing the train to a full and sudden stop is going to be harsh on the train and its contents. It is going to send cargo flying and jostling about. It is ill-advised. So, what do you do instead of stopping that negative train on a dime? Gently, slowly, ease up on the momentum. Bring the train to a slow roll. Eventually, to a gentle stop. When you are ready, you can let your train rest in neutral for as long as it feels good to be there. Finally, when it feels right, you can point the train in a new direction and slowly pull away, gaining steady momentum, naturally, safely, and comfortably.

To accomplish this with the momentum of thought, you must first recognize the direction you are going and do not chastise yourself for it. In fact, you should congratulate yourself for being brave enough to take an objective look at your own thought patterns. Once you recognize the train is headed in a direction that feels less than good and looks less than productive, you can practice thought exercises that will slow the momentum on the negative thoughts by getting general and going neutral.

Slowing Down a Fast-Moving Train

Let us look at an example of how it is possible to slow down a thought-train headed in the wrong direction with strong momentum.

This will give us a better overall understanding of how positive thinking works and how we can use it to benefit our own healthy development. We will take the example of an average individual waiting for a job offer they have been hoping for. In a moment of doubt, the individual gives attention to the following idea:

- I won't get this job

The subconscious mind begins to imagine what that will be like. It spins a little tangent about the moment the individual finds out he or she didn't get the job…how much time and effort it will be to keep looking for another job…what it feels like to be defeated again. The train has left the station and it is heading in a negative direction. Soon, other thoughts join that first one:

- I won't get this job
- My interview could have gone better
- Other applicants are better than me
- I never get the jobs I want
- I should have tried harder
- I should have dressed differently
- I should have answered differently
- I always sabotage myself

In less than 60 seconds of thought, the momentum has built steadily in the negative direction. As these thoughts continue to gain momentum in the wrong direction, the subconscious mind is listening and believing the story, it is being told. The subconscious mind believes the story so much that it starts to generate emotions based on that story. The individual begins to feel sad, cheated, doubtful and used.

Now that the subconscious mind believes the story, it shares this information with other parts of the mind that control what the body is physically feeling. As these negative ideas and stories are repeated to the subconscious mind, the body begins to act in accordance with these stories, too. If the individual repeats thoughts and stories that reiterate feelings of exhaustion, anxiety, and fear, the body physiologically begins to experience these symptoms. The individual may begin to feel fatigued in the body. Muscles and joints may become stiff and sore or tight where stress is held in the body. Feelings of anxiety can cause the body to start feeling panicked, even leading to an actual panic attack just from thinking negative thoughts.

With all this momentum behind the train, how is the individual supposed to stop it safely? The idea is to take the first offending statement and make it more neutral and less negative, but still something the individual actually believes. That is to say, it is rather impossible for the individual to lie to him or herself. The individual cannot just change the sentence from, "I won't get this job"; to "I know I've got the job!" Chances are the individual will not readily believe they will have the job, so the positive phrase is only more of an antagonize and sarcastic reminder of not getting the job. Instead of antagonizing oneself, the individual can practice a less specific, more neutral, but still believable statement.

The individual may change the thought: I will not get this job

To the thought: I do not know if I am going to get this job

Already, there is less stress and pain in the statement. It is true, the individual does not yet know whether they were chosen for the job, so logically, this statement is sound; it is believable. It is also not as negative and hurtful; it is not so final.

Now the individual may go forward from that statement and propose another general, neutral, better-feeling idea. Alternatively, the momentum of the negative train might be so strong that the individual is pulled back in that direction. That too is okay. When it happens, the individual can simply acknowledge it has happened, and get general and neutral again.

Let us see some more examples of how the individual can use this positive thinking tactically to slow down negative thoughts and bring the train into neutral:

- I won't get this job → I don't know if I'm going to get this job

- My interview could have gone better → Some parts of that interview went really well

- Other applicants are better than me → I have the experience and the desire for this job

- I never get the jobs I want → I've really liked a couple of the jobs I've had

- I should've tried harder → I did what I could do and that's enough

- I should've dressed differently → I dressed respectfully and professionally

- I should've answered differently → That one answer I gave was a big hit

- I always sabotage myself → If I get the job good and if not, good

The adjusted thoughts are still true for the individual, but they also feel better to think and they do not give the negative thought-train more power to sustain its momentum. When the individual replaces negative thoughts with those that feel less resistant; less stressful, less painful, the momentum of the negative train slows down.

It is as if the individual stops shoveling coal into that train's fire. It has not given the fuel it needs to run, so the train begins to slow down.

If you continue to practice positive and deliberate thinking, then the momentum of this negative thought-train will eventually roll to a neutral. A thought-train can be brought to a neutral place by practicing the shifting of ideas from non-serving, to serving; from negative to neutral (or positive). Watch our same trigger phrase move up the scale, from feeling bad to feeling good for the individual to think about and repeat.

- I will not get this job.

- I never get the jobs I want.

- I do not know if I will get this job.

- At least once or twice, I have landed the job I wanted.

- It is possible I could get this job.

- I would not have made it to the interview round if I were not qualified.

- I would be very good at this job.

- I can see myself at this job.

- I can see myself liking this job.

- I have many ideas to bring to this job.

- I have the experience or the drive for this job.

- It is a good thing if I get this job.

- It is a good thing if I do not get this job because the perfect job is coming.

- Even if I do not get this job, I have already learned so much.

- The next time I interview, I will be even better.

- I would be happy with this job or not.

- I am so proud of myself for applying to this job.

- I am a perfect fit for this job.

- This job would fit really well with my other goals and cares.

- This job, or a job like it, is meant for me.

- I will get this job.

With a short amount of words and time, the individual has softened him or herself on the subject of the job. No statement went harshly against the individual's core beliefs, and each neutralizing thought brings the individual's thought-train to a slow.

When you first begin to practice this technique of shifting ideas and internal stories in order to slow the train, it can feel a bit rusty. This may especially be the case if your wheels have been practicing turning one way for a long while. When you start to turn the wheels the other way, it is a mostly unused motion. It will take a few minutes to knock the dust off it and get it going. However, if your mind is capable of sending ideas speeding down a track in one direction, it can do the same in another direction. A positive and deliberate direction.

Be easy on yourself when practicing this and remember there is no such truth as doing it wrong. If you find yourself back to the familiar old negative thought patterns, it is ok. It is even natural for that to happen. Acknowledge it, put yourself facing the positive direction again, and return to building that momentum. Eventually, the train that is given the most attention and energy is the train with the stronger momentum.

There is a simple way to tell if a thought is serving you, or tormenting you: how it feels.

- "I hate everyone" ... feels pretty bad

- "I love everyone" ...feels untrue and mocking, so still feels bad

- "There is one person I don't hate in the world" ...less friction in that statement

- "There may even be two people in the world I don't hate" ... less friction in that statement

- "I don't hate everyone" ... less friction in that statement

- "Some people are ok" ... less friction in that statement

- "That one guy a particular time was good" ...feeling better

- "That person from history did some stuff I like" ...less friction

- "This person alive now does stuff like that, too" ... feeling better

- "It's nice to know at least a couple of good people" ...feeling better

- "I hate that person who made me mad still" ... more friction in that statement

- "But at least I know this good person over here" ... less friction

- "I have respect for this person" ... feeling better

- "But I still hate that one person" ... more friction again

- "But at least I don't have to see that person anymore" ...less friction

And so on, you go; fine-tuning your thoughts deliberately.

Chapter 7 Remove Negative Influences

Everybody needs to carry on with a progressively positive life, however, there are constantly negative impacts that are attempting to stop you. They may originate all things considered or from inside you. Any place they originate from, there are many things that placed marks in your inspiration, self-assurance, and joy. It could be a companion or relative who appears to be just to condemn you, or it could be a terrible propensity that you cannot shake.

Step by step instructions to cut negative influences from your life and be a more positive person

Negative idea examples are a thing that can keep you down when you cannot resist the urge to expect the most noticeably awful constantly. Be that as it may, you do not need these terrible impacts to govern your life. On the off chance that you need to prevent them from controlling you, you have to remove them. In any case, this is not a simple activity, so do not give it a chance to get you down in the event that you cannot change as long as you can remember in multi-day. Pursue these means to dispose of the negative impacts throughout your life and begin living all the more decidedly.

Changing Your Lifestyle

Other individuals aren't the main thing that can massively

affect your life. It is exceptionally simple to get into negative behavior patterns that become decision impacts. When you take a gander at your way of life, you can find that you are reliant on something that has begun managing how you live. In the event that you admit to and attempt to deal with these addictions, you can turn into a more joyful and increasingly sure individual. It does not make a difference in the event that you have to get liquor enslavement treatment, change your association with sustenance or go on an innovation detox. Nothing should run your life such that makes you have a feeling that you need to do it, regardless of whether it is created you troubled. Change these destructive impacts to great ones, for example, heaps of various interests, exercise, and mingling.

In the event that you need to begin thinking all the more decidedly, there are different pieces of your way of life you can change. At the point when your conditions are making you think adversely, it tends to be much simpler to transform them than to change yourself. In the event that your activity is making you miserable and you keep failing, begin searching for another one. Address the things that are controlling your life and get the chance to chip away at how you are going to make things not the same as now on.

Encircle Yourself with Positive People

The general population we invest our energy with, just as

the ones we must choose the option to see, can tremendously affect us. You can start to disguise other individuals' voices, as you begin to accept the frightful things they state. You can most likely consider in any event one individual in your life who consistently leaves you longing that you hadn't got together with them. Here and there the best activity about them is to expel them from your life. Be that as it may, you aren't constantly ready. A few people in your family or at work are unavoidable. In this way, just as cutting off negative associations, you ought to likewise figure out how to manage them and offset them out with progressively positive ones.

In the event that you conclude that you are in an ideal situation without somebody, ensure that you are sure this is the correct advance. This intense move is hard to return from, and you probably won't most likely fix your relationship. Cutting somebody from your life is simpler to do if it is a companion. You do not need to appear them, as you do your family, or to associate with other people who know them. It is totally up to you whether you keep a companion around. Obviously, you likewise get the chance to pick on the off chance that you need a relative in your life. Simply make certain that you are making the correct move to remove somebody who is unfeeling, damaging or careless.

Some antagonistic individuals are unavoidable.

Possibly you have associates you cannot coexist with, your closest companion's irritating accomplice or a basic relative you need to see during the occasions. When you cannot expel somebody from your life, or choose not to, you can figure out how to manage them all the more emphatically. On the off chance that you do not, you could wind up giving their sentiments a chance to influence your life. There are heaps of ways you can manage the kind of individual who just appears to have awful things to state. One of them is just to grin and segregate yourself, disregarding what they let you know. Be that as it may, you cannot utilize this strategy in certain spots, for example, at work. When you have to remain connected with others, attempt to get them to offset out their considerations with positive explanations. Make sure to concentrate without anyone else vitality, and remind yourself that their pessimism is their concern.

When you are compelled to have antagonistic individuals throughout your life, ensure you offset them out with increasingly positive impacts. Encircle yourself with constructive individuals and avert other individuals' antagonism with your inspiration.

Step by step instructions to cut negative influences from your life and be a more positive person

You cannot dispose of negative contemplations or circumstances through and through, however, you can concentrate on the beneficial things. You can remove a positive from anything that transpires, regardless of how little.

Perhaps you had a horrendous day, yet somebody was

benevolent enough to hold an entryway open for you when you got the chance to work. So you haven't figured out how to lose any weight for some time – however, you have opposed allurement and dodged the no-go sustenance in your eating regimen plan. Positive thinking is tied in with praising the beneficial things and battle the terrible by not giving it a chance to govern your life.

Battling Negative Thinking

You can possibly change your way of life in the event that you think in an increasingly positive manner, and manage negative contemplations appropriately. Keeping away from antagonistic individuals assists with this, yet you additionally need to glimpse further inside yourself. Probably the best activity to improve your life is to define objectives and points, so you have something to pursue. Be that as it may, you have to take a gander at your idea examples to enable you to remain on track. When you are thinking contrarily, you should see where your considerations and sentiments are originating from to enable you to get to the base of the issue.

Chapter 8 Strategies for Ending Overthinking

Now that you are aware of how you can identify your overthinking behaviors, and how you can identify what is causing them, you need to start becoming aware of how you can actually shift your overthinking behaviors when they arise. In the beginning, one of the most effective tools that you can equip yourself with is one that can support you in ending an episode of overthinking behaviors as they begin. This is because you are likely so used to overthinking at this point that completely preventing episodes of overthinking is highly unlikely; your brain is wired to behave this way when certain triggers are being pulled and rewiring it takes time. Knowing how to put a stop to your overthinking in the moment will not only support you with ending that specific episode of overthinking, but also with eliminating your likelihood of overthinking again in the future by training your brain to respond differently.

There are many things that you can do to eliminate overthinking from your life, depending on what you are overthinking about and what emotions are arising as a result of your overthinking.

The most important part in developing a strategy for overcoming overthinking is committing to one or two strategies that fit your needs and using those strategies every single time you experience an episode. It is important that you maintain consistency in your strategy because you want to rewire your brain to effectively work through overthinking episodes, which is accomplished through repetition.

Below, you have been given six different strategies that you can use to help you combat your overthinking behaviors. Each strategy has been accompanied with who it will work best for, how you can use it, and why it is going to support you in overcoming overthinking. Read through each of them so that you can understand how they work and who they are meant for, and then pick two or three strategies that you can use to help you begin overcoming overthinking. Once you have committed to the ones you want to test, you can begin using them right away anytime you find yourself overthinking. Remember, you want to use them every single time you become aware of your overthinking behaviors so that you can train your brain to respond differently to this ineffective thought pattern.

Ground Yourself

Grounding is a strategy that can support virtually anyone in overcoming overthinking behaviors by providing you with the opportunity to center yourself and refocus on the topic at hand. This is particularly helpful for anyone who may be overthinking due to fear or anxiety, as these emotional responses can influence an individual to feel as though they are losing control of the situation. Grounding will support you in regaining control over yourself and your responses so that you can feel confident in approaching any task at hand with the cognition and awareness that you need to be successful with it.

Grounding works by giving you a few moments to take back control over your responses to an experience that you are having in life that may be causing you to feel nervous or like you are overthinking. When you ground, you bring your awareness back to your body and your mind so that you can recall that you are the one in control over your thoughts and behaviors in any situation, and that your emotions do not have the capacity to run the show without your permission. When you take back control in this way, rationally using your mind to monitor and adjust your thoughts is a lot easier, thus enabling you to feel more empowered to make the necessary decisions to maintain your comfort and safety.

From an overthinking perspective, knowing that you have the capacity to be in control over your thoughts and emotions using the power of your rational brain means that you no longer have to feel as though you are being hijacked by your emotional responses to certain triggers.

If you are a naturally curious person, this means that you no longer have to be hijacked by your curiosity which could cause you to begin overthinking and procrastinating.

If you experience anxiety, this means no longer being hijacked by fear and intrusive thoughts which can lead to overthinking and an increase in your fear and stress response to certain triggers. As a result, you are able to intentionally decide how you will respond to various experiences in your life, rather than feeling as though you are being forced to behave based in a certain way on your automatic emotional responses. This means that if you overthink to attempt to gain more information or feel in control, you will no longer need to overthink because your confidence in being able to gain the right information and control the situation is fulfilled.

Grounding can be done in just a few minutes, making it a great practice to use on the go or in virtually any situation that you may face in your life. You can ground in the lineup at the supermarket, in your car in the parking lot, across the table from your date, or while you are sitting at home after a particularly stressful day. The best thing about grounding is that it can be done in a number of different ways, depending on what feels best for you. Below are two different grounding strategies that you can use: one that takes only a moment and one that takes slightly longer. Both of these strategies are powerful in helping you ground, so you will want to pick the one that suits you best and use that one.

The first grounding strategy that you can try takes only a few moments.

It works simply: all you need to do is plant your two feet on the ground and envision your connection to the Earth existing through your feet. As you do, begin repeating affirmations to yourself that help you feel more confident and in control during challenging experiences. You can design your own affirmations that fit your unique needs when it comes to grounding, or you can use the following affirmations to help you:

- "I am grounded and safe."
- "I am confident."
- "I can do this."
- "I accept myself unconditionally."
- "I can find the solution with ease."

The second grounding strategy that you can use is common when it comes to the world of psychology, as many psychologists suggest it as being one of the most powerful grounding techniques that a person with anxiety or overthinking behaviors can use.

This strategy requires you to infuse your five senses with the experience that you are having so that you can begin feeling more connected to your physical body and environment. You start by looking at five different things and mentally describing these things to yourself, for example: "Green curtain, yellow cup, purple fountain, white couch, and brown book."

Next, you want to touch four different things that provide you with different sensations to experience through your physical touch. Try and touch things with different textures so that you can stay focused on each individual thing that you are touching. If you are going to be in an environment where you do not have the ability to start randomly touching things, consider wearing clothes or jewelry that has different textures so that you can simply touch your outfit for this part. Next, you want to find three different things that you can listen to and you want to mentally describe where they are coming from, for example: "Crying baby, traffic from the street, and beeping from the kitchen." Then, you want to find two different things that you can smell, or notice two separate scents from your environment. If you can, you can start smelling flowers, perfumes, colognes, candles, or anything else that may be scented in your environment. If not, you might consider attempting to describe the scent of your environment to yourself and then smelling your own perfume, or even a small bottle of essential oils that you keep in your purse. Finally, you want to describe one thing that you can taste. This one tends to be hardest, as you may not be able to describe any specific taste if you have not eaten or drink anything recently. If this is the case, you can always carry gum or mints in your purse so that you can pop one in your mouth and describe the taste to yourself as you chew it.

This particular strategy may sound time consuming, but once you start it should only take a couple of minutes for you to move through each of your senses and bring your awareness back into your body. The biggest benefit of this strategy is that not only will it help ground you but it will also help distract you from the overthinking behaviors that are causing you to feel stuck in your head or removed from your physical environment. The more you distract and ground yourself in this way, the easier it will be for you to regain control over your mind and distract yourself from unhealthy overthinking behaviors when they arise.

Reframe Your Thoughts

Often, the thoughts you are having can directly contribute to you feeling trapped in an overthinking process whereby it feels as though you cannot help but stay trapped in your thoughts.

The reality is: feeding your overthinking behaviors with more overthinking is never helpful, but when we are being consumed by emotions that lead us to believe that our overthinking patterns are normal, it can be easy to feed your behaviors with more worrying thoughts. Learning how to reframe your thoughts to take you out of the position of the victim or a state of distraction so that you can put yourself in charge of any situation that you are involved in is a powerful way to overcoming overthinking behaviors and create a more productive mindset.

Reframing your thoughts is best for individuals who are experiencing feelings of fear or anxiety that are causing them to overthink about the experiences that they are having. If you find that you are overthinking due to stress or worrying experiences, chances are you need to reframe your thoughts so that you can feel more in control over the experiences that you are having.

Reframing is a simple practice where you essentially audit the thoughts that you are having and change the way that you are thinking about them so that you can see yourself and your situation through a different perspective. Remember, the thoughts you have contribute to your emotions, so if you are thinking disempowering thoughts you are going to start feeling disempowered and this is going to lead to you feeling as though you cannot achieve what you aspire to accomplish. Alternatively, if you begin thinking about everything except the solution, you are going to begin feeling emotions of curiosity and wonder rather than emotions of focus and determination. While no feelings are technically "bad" feelings, experiencing feelings out of turn or in excessive amounts can lead to any individual feeling as though they cannot reasonably accomplish what they need to in order to navigate a situation that would typically trigger overthinking behaviors.

Reframing your thoughts starts by auditing your thoughts and considering how they might be disempowering you or leaving you feeling as though you are unworthy or uncapable of doing something. For example, if you are thinking thoughts of "I can't do this" you know that these words specifically lead to you feeling disempowered because you are speaking against your skills and abilities, thus leaving you feeling like you are not capable enough.

You know, then, that the word "can't" is directly responsible for how you are feeling and is likely the reason for why your thoughts are leading to an increase in unwanted emotions.

In order to reframe this thought, you need to consider what

it is that you are wanting to feel and then generate a thought that will help you feel that way. For example, maybe you think "I can't do this" because you presently lack the skills required to complete a task, so you believe that you are incapable of accomplishing what you desire to accomplish based on this lack of skills. However, if you know that you want to do said thing, or if it is necessary for you to do it, then you are going to need to acquire the skill in order to be able to create the results that you desire. This means that you are going to need to generate emotions of motivation and determination, by adjusting your thoughts to something like "I can learn" or "I can find a way." These thoughts are far more empowering and will motivate you to start feeling capable and confident, thus enabling you to feel empowered to take the necessary actions to move forward.

You can reframe any thought that is not serving you simply by getting to the root of what that thought is causing you to experience emotionally and how you can change that thought so that you can experience more positive or productive emotions. Below are some examples of reframed thoughts that you can use to help you understand how reframing works and feel inspired to begin reframing your own thoughts when you are being overwhelmed with overthinking behaviors.

- ***"I am not good enough"*** creates feelings of unworthiness, "I am valuable" creates feelings of worthiness.
- ***"I am too inexperienced"*** creates feelings of not being capable, "I can learn more" creates feelings of empowerment to increase your experience.
- ***"No one ever likes me"*** creates feelings of being disliked and unwanted, "My Mom, brother, sister, and Grandma all like me" creates feelings of being liked and wanted by people who matter to you.
- ***"I am too awkward to date"*** creates feelings of fear around dating, "I am learning how to be myself on dates" creates a feeling of empowerment around being yourself when dating.
- ***"My boss does not like me"*** creates a feeling of negativity and resentment around your work, "I am good at what I do" creates a feeling of empowerment and confidence around your work.

In addition to reframing specific negative thoughts, you can also reframe an overall thinking pattern. For example, say you are preparing to go on a date with someone for the first time and you begin overthinking about your looks, what you are going to say, how you are going to behave, and how you are going to impress this person.

Naturally, you do not want to sit and reframe every single thought as this will likely not be effective. Instead, you want to get to the root of what your overall thinking is causing you to feel or believe about yourself so that you can counter that belief. Typically, overthinking about trying to impress someone or be liked by someone is driven by a fear of not being good enough or likeable as you are. In that case, you would want to reframe this entire thought process with simple yet powerful affirmations like "I am good enough" and "I like me for who I am." These types of affirmations counter the negative thoughts that are beneath the overall pattern that you are experiencing, which supports you in eliminating overthinking behaviors by eliminating the root cause of them.

Distract Yourself

If you are someone who overthinks because you are consistently curious about the things going on around you, learning how to use distraction as a method to stop you from overthinking is a powerful strategy. You can use distraction to help you stop overthinking anytime you find that you are being distracted by unproductive thoughts that are either keeping you from being able to achieve the task at hand, or keeping you from being comfortable in your environment.

Distraction is quite simple, and it can be done either through thoughts or through action depending on why you are overthinking and what situation you are presently experiencing.

If you are overthinking because you are curious, so you find yourself asking unnecessary questions or seeking unnecessary answers to the situation that you are experiencing, distracting yourself through thoughts followed by immediate action is important. You can do this by identifying what your area of focus needs to be and then taking action to help you commit to that area of focus. For example, say you need to focus so that you can get work done but you find yourself continually being carried away by your overthinking behaviors. Instead of allowing yourself to continue overthinking, you can think about what needs to be accomplished right in this minute to keep you productive and then take action toward completing that. For example, say you have a report that needs to be accomplished for your boss by 3:00 PM but it is 1:00 PM and you cannot seem to stay focused on the report. Instead of focusing and getting your work done, you are overthinking and remaining unproductive, which means that you have less and less time left to finish it. In this situation, you would want to distract yourself from overthinking by asking yourself what one thing you could do in this moment to begin finishing the report on time, and then immediately you want to get started on working toward that one thing. This way, you can distract yourself from your distractions and stay physically invested in what needs to get done. Anytime you find yourself overthinking or growing distracted by your thoughts again, you could use this strategy to regain your focus and proceed.

If you are overthinking because you are worried or afraid of something, distracting yourself from your feelings of worry or fear is a great opportunity for you to begin overcoming your overthinking patterns and staying focused. You can do this by distracting yourself with reasons why you are happy or excited to be doing what it is that you are about to do, or by distracting yourself with something different entirely. For example, say you are overthinking because you have an important test to do in the morning and you are afraid that you are not prepared enough for that test. Rationally, you know that you have studied every day for months and that you know the information better than anyone else in your class so there is absolutely no reason for you to fail that particular test. Still, you cannot help but feel afraid that you are going to mess up in some way and as a result you are going to have to retake the entire class, so your worrying thoughts begin to increase to the point that you are now overthinking. Instead of investing yourself in these thoughts, you could do one of two things: study if you genuinely believe that you are not ready, or engage in something else entirely to take your mind off of the test. If you are confident in your knowledge, completely distracting yourself from the test altogether is a positive way to make sure that you are allowing your brain the opportunity to destress from the topic of the test and enjoy something else for a change. You could watch movies, spend some time with a friend, read a book, or even cook yourself a nice meal all to help distract yourself from that which you are worried about.

Distracting yourself from the unproductive thoughts that are causing problems for you is a powerful way to interrupt the overthinking process and begin engaging in healthier thought patterns. This way, instead of being overwhelmed by thoughts that are preventing you from focusing or that are causing you to feel like you are not good enough, you can begin focusing on something more productive, like the work that needs to get done or things that make you feel happier. When it comes to psychological patterns, this supports you in interrupting present thought loops so that you can begin training your brain to respond to triggers in a different way. In essence, it is a powerful self-disciplinary tool that can support you in regaining control over your brain so that you can feel more successful in your life.

Use A Timer

Sometimes, overthinking is inevitable and you are going to overthink whether you intend to or not. Overthinking is a behavior that may arise as a result of you needing to think something through or process some form of information that is being brought to your attention through triggers and thoughts that are causing you to overthink.

If this is the case, learning how to set limitations on and boundaries around your overthinking behaviors is a great opportunity for you to engage in the necessary thought processes without being completely overcome by them. Setting boundaries with yourself is not only going to teach you how to stop overthinking, but it is also going to teach you how to respect the word "no" or "done" when you say it.

This strategy for overcoming overthinking behaviors is powerful no matter what your reason for overthinking is, as it can support you in taking control in any situation. You can use the process of setting boundaries and time limits on your overthinking behaviors on the go or when you are at home, or you can even incorporate it into your day to day routine as a preventative measure to support you in keeping your mind free and clear during the day. If you use this strategy on a regular basis, you should know that your biggest goal here will not be to overcome overthinking behaviors completely, but instead gain control over them so that you are no longer being taken over by your overthinking behaviors.

The easiest way to set yourself up for success with this pattern is to set a timer on your phone or even set a standard kitchen timer and allow yourself complete freedom to overthink for that entire period of time. If you are in a rush, you can give yourself one or two minutes, or if you have longer you can give yourself a five- or ten-minute thinking break so that you can process through all of the thoughts that are keeping you distracted. Once your timer goes off, keep yourself focused on the task at hand so that you are no longer being distracted by your overthinking thoughts. Anytime you notice yourself becoming distracted again, you can simply say "no thank you" and then return your attention to the task that you are working on.

If you want to use this strategy as a preventative measure to stop you from overthinking, you will want to do so by using both a journal and a timer and then sitting down and free writing all of your thoughts for a set period of time. Doing this once per day, either in the morning before you start the day or in the evening before you go to bed, is a powerful way to make sure that you are continually getting all of your excess thoughts out of your mind so that you are no longer being overwhelmed by them. Writing down your thoughts is the key, even if you just write them down in bullet point or in a completely irrational order, because it helps you actually remove the thoughts from your mind and allows you to feel as though they have been processed more completely. As a result, you will find that it is easier for you to avoid overthinking throughout the day because you have given yourself a set period of time where you can complete your overthinking behaviors each day. Your mind begins to grow accustomed to having this opportunity and, as a result, setting boundaries with yourself during the day becomes easier because you can rationally look forward to a period of time each day where these thoughts will be addressed.

Chapter 9 The Magic of Mindfulness

Let's say you are at a job interview. Of course, you're nervous because you want the job. But rather than being completely present and attentive to what is going on, what do most of us tend to do in situations like these? We let our minds go on a spree of negative thoughts. We think back to previous interviews that didn't go well. We look for signs in the interviewer's behavior to see whether he is impressed. We jump ahead to the future, thinking, "I bet there are a lot of applicants more qualified than I. This is a waste of time; or "Why did I say that? He doesn't look too impressed". Or simply, "I'll probably get rejected". In short, you are only half present at that interview. Part of your mind is there while the other part is going off on totally different tangents. This is a familiar scenario in so many different situations because we have not learned to be mindful.

Here is another scenario that might be familiar: Many of us pride ourselves on multi-tasking. We talk on the phone while checking our emails and making to-do lists. We fold laundry while watching TV and keeping an eye on the casserole cooking on the oven.

We have a hasty lunch at our office desk while going over reports... and then we wonder why we feel so exhausted and burned out at the end of the day.

We are not practicing mindfulness. Multi-tasking is not proof of how capable we are. The only thing it does is scatter our thoughts – and mindfulness requires a fully-focused mind.

All human beings are born with the quality of mindfulness but many of us have lost it along the way. This is good news. It means that we don't have to create mindfulness because it's we already have it; it's innate to human beings. Therefore, through proven practices and techniques, we can easily train the mind to cultivate it. This chapter will teach you how to do that.,

Mindfulness is absolutely key to rewiring the mind, it is absolutely key for the wellbeing and peace pf mind that so many people lack. It can be defined as:

- The total awareness of the mind to what is happening at the present moment; where you are, what you are doing and what is happening.
- The ability to be fully present at the moment with total neutrality. That is, without being overly reactive or judgmental towards what is happening.
- It is the attentive observation of our thoughts and feelings at a given moment, without labeling them as good or bad but simply experiencing them.
- In a nutshell, mindfulness means "being present".

How does it work?

Mindfulness has its earliest roots in Buddhism, but most religions incorporate some form of mindfulness practices as well, such as prayer or meditation to promote spiritual calm and mindful awareness.

Mindfulness techniques are becoming more widely practiced in psychotherapy as an alternative to medication because just like medication, mindfulness can help people develop a more rational perspective on harmful behaviors and negative, self-defeating thoughts. Experts believe that mindfulness helps us become more accepting of our negative experiences rather than reacting to them with irrational behavior.

Losing touch with ourselves and with reality

Mindfulness may seem trivial – and easy - at first glance but nothing could be farther from the truth. It is a very profound concept because like in the previous interview example above, unless we train our brain to be mindful, it will veer off on different tangents - usually negative ones - causing us to lose touch with reality.

We are too busy reliving things that have already happened, or worrying about the future, when there's nothing we can do about either. In the case of multi-tasking, we are again missing out on the present moment because our brain is trying to cope with several things at once.

The following quote by Buddha sums it up perfectly: "The secret of health for both mind and body are not to mourn for the past, worry about the future or anticipate trouble, but to live I the present moment wisely and earnestly".

Benefits of mindfulness

When we live mindfully, we ultimately become the best of who we are as human beings. Mindfulness brings out a multitude of wonderful qualities in us that we never knew existed. Some benefits of mindfulness include:

- In the workplace, mindfulness helps reduce stress, improve relationships with colleagues and boost productivity.
- It improves personal relationships. Interacting mindfully with your partner or children builds mutual love, trust and appreciation because you become more attentive and non-judgmental in your conversations.
- If mindfulness becomes a way of life, it can be totally transformative. If it becomes more than just a practice, if you commit to making it part of your nature, it will bring heightened awareness and caring to everything you do.
- Mindfulness teaches you to be less critical and more compassionate and accepting of yourself. You learn to catch and stop negative thoughts before they become patterns.

- Studies have shown that practicing mindfulness prevents depression, anxiety and stress and that if they do arise, you are able to overcome them. Over time, mindfulness creates inner peace, a sense of wellbeing and happiness.
- Mindfulness has been shown to improve memory and creativity.
- Mindfulness helps us identify deep buried past emotions that may be harming our career and relationships.
- Research has shown that by reducing stress and anxiety, mindfulness can improve overall health and reduce the risk of stress-related illnesses like high blood pressure. Studies have also shown that it can relieve chronic pain and gastrointestinal disorders, as well as improve sleep.

10 Simple Mindfulness Exercises for Beginners

Exercise 1: Mindful Breathing

This exercise can be done standing up or sitting down, so it's ideal to do when you're waiting in line for something.

- Inhale slowly through your nose as you count to 6

- Exhale through your mouth while counting to 6
- Let your thoughts go, block out any sounds or activity going on around you. Focus only on your breath, feel it as it enters and leaves your body. Be aware of it passing through your nose and into your lungs, then passing out of your lungs through your mount
- Repeat 10 times

Thus, us a great exercise for calming the mind in the middle of a hectic workday or when you have the jitters before a public speech or presentation.

Exercise 2: Hand Awareness Technique

- Intertwine the fingers of both hands together and clench as hard as you can for 5-10 seconds then release.
- Be aware of how your hands feel as you are clenching them and when you release them. Focus on the tension in your fingers and palms as you clench and the feeling of release when you let go.

Exercise 3: Observation Technique

Despite its simplicity, this exercise is incredibly powerful for increasing your perception, awareness and appreciation of the everyday things around you. It really helps clear and calm the mind during hectic times.

- Choose something natural in your environment to focus on, such as a tree outside your office window, flowers, a butterfly, a cloud or a star in the sky.
  - Observe every aspect if the object as if you're seeing it for the first time; its shape, color, and movement, as if seeing it for the first time. Feel its energy and connect with it.
  - Relax your mind and just observe the object for as long as you can concentrate.

Exercise 4: Body Sensation Exercise

- Sit very still and become aware of your body; the feeling of your hands in your lap, your feet touching the floor and any other sensation such as an itch.
- Start with your head and gradually move down your body, becoming aware of each part, until you reach your toes.

Exercise 5: Heightened Awareness of Everyday Things

A great exercise to heighten your awareness of everyday things and tasks that we take for granted.

- Choose a simple daily task that you perform every day, such as stirring sugar into your tea, sending an SMS message or even something as mundane as opening and closing a door.
- The moment you start performing the task, become mindful of what you're doing. Be aware of the aroma of

your tea, the spoon moving in a circular motion and the feel of the spoon un your hand, and so on.
- Then, think of how delicious your tea will taste, or the person who will receive your SMS message, or where the door you are opening will lead you.
- Another example you smell food cooking in your kitchen. Savor the smell and be grateful for the good meal you are going to have.
- Nothing is too small or mundane to go unnoticed. Schedule half an hour of your day to become aware of every simple task you do and to be grateful.

Exercise 6: Sensory Mindfulness Practice

This exercise heightens our mindfulness of taste, touch, smell and hearing to the simple things around us, grounding our mind in the present moment.

- Stop at any moment of the day and with your senses, become aware of whatever it is you are doing.
- Feel anything you are holding in your hands and become aware of its weight and texture.
- Become aware of any sounds around you; voices, a car horn, the TV, the buzz of conversation in a café or restaurant, etc.
- Become aware of any smells
- The simple task if washing dishes is a good example, where you can focus on the feel of running water on your hands, its warmth, the feel of the sponge and the dishes.

Then, listen to the sound of the running water and smell the dishwashing liquid.

Exercise 7: Emotional Mindfulness

- Pause what you are doing for a few moments and become aware of how you feel.
- Simply observe how you feel without judgment or reaction.
- Label your emotions at that moment; joy, frustration, anger, pleasure, etc.
- Continue to be aware of the emotions for a few moments then disengage your mind and continue with what you were doing.

Exercise 8: Urge Mindfulness Technique

This is a great one for substance addictions as it helps strengthen your commitment to overcome them.

- Allow your mind to acknowledge a craving when it comes up without passing any judgment on it or on yourself
- Become aware of your sensations when the urge or craving comes up
- Become certain in your mind that it will subside.
- Allow the urge or craving to pass.

Exercise 9: Mindful Listening

- Sit in a relaxed position with eyes closed and listen to your favorite song.

- Become mindful of the emotions it stirs up in you. Observe them without judging and let them pass
- Become mindful of any memories it brings up, and let them pass.

Exercise 10: Mindful Immersion

- Relax for a few moments and imagine yourself slowly merging into everything around you
- Imagine the atoms of our busy expanding out and fusing with all the objects around you.
- With practice, this exercise will help you feel at one with the world and develop inner peace.

The aim of these exercises is to help you become aware of the present as it is, and to release any judgments or emotions that arise. The aim of mindfulness as a whole is not to relax or calm the mind but to live in the immediate present.

You will have difficulty keeping your mind focused, especially if you're a chronic multi-tasker. But I can promise you that with daily practice, you will get results, and you will be amazed.

Mindfulness meditation

Are you one of those people who think meditation is just not for them? Well, think again. The previous exercises were nothing more than mini meditations!

There are many different types of meditation but mindfulness mediation did not become known in the western world until recently. Tidy, it is used by many psychologists to supplement various treatments for depression, obsessive-compulsive disorders and addiction.

Mindfulness meditations differ from mindfulness exercises in that they are longer and would require a scheduled time and a quiet space, but the goal is the same.

Before you start

- Schedule time for your meditation when you will not be interrupted
- Select a quiet space or environment where you feel comfortable
- Choose a sitting position where you will not feel uncomfortable after a time. You can sit on a cushion on the floor, or in a comfortable chair or a park bench; whatever works best for you.
- Go with the flow. When you meditate, don't try to judge or push away any thoughts or emotions that come to you. Just flow with them, observe them and let them pass.

Additional tips for practicing mindfulness

1. ***Concentration is key.*** I know that this is easier said than done. If you are new to mindfulness techniques, your

mind will frequently wander. If it does, just bring your concentration back to the exercise and continue, or even start over if you have the time. It is key that you do this rather than think, "My mind can't concentrate right now, I'll do it another time" Remember, you are in control not your mind. When you continue to draw it back to the task at hand, it will gradually learn to remain anchored. Over time, you will easily be able to transition into mindful observation, mindful walking, mindful eating and mindful conversation.

2. ***Choose easy objects.*** Rather than focusing on a whole tree, for example, start simple at first. A pencil or a coffee mug, a flower or a leaf, and so on. Rather than concentrating on smalls and sounds, start with just one sound or one smell. Continue to do this for a week or two then move to more complex objects, hearing and smell together, then hearing. Smells and sensations. Take all the time you need until you feel ready to transition from one stage to the other.

3. ***Don't rush.*** Trying to rush mindfulness is not going to get you anywhere. Remember, you are undoing years of living in the past or the future rather than in the present and retraining your mind to abandon those od pathways requires time and patience.

4. **Practice while sitting down.** Do your exercises while sitting down at first to ease and relax your mind.
5. **Redirect when meditating or practicing.** If you find your mind wandering to the pile of laundry waiting to be washed or that report you have to hand in, take note of where your thoughts are going and gently redirect your mind back to the present moment.
6. **Don't give up.** If you miss your meditation or something disturbs you during mindfulness practice, schedule a new meditation or start the exercise again.
7. **Cultivate "spur of the moment" mindfulness.** Don't rely solely on formal meditation and exercises to cultivate mindfulness. Try to be as mindful whenever you can as you go about your daily routine, whether it is mopping the kitchen floor, feeding your cat, climbing a flight of stairs or walking through the parking lot to our office. Every single thing you do is an opportunity to be mindful so get creative and discover these new opportunities. Let it become your way of life!
8. **Be fully committed.** If you want to become mindful, you need to make it a priority. Daily practice is essential to break those old habits and start creating a mindful mind. Remember, you are in a conflict with your mind, which will try to pull you back to the old habits. The more you "push back" and the more often you practice, the lesser your mind's pull on you will become.

9. **_Make it a daily practice._** All you need is 5 minutes during your lunch break for a short meditation or mindfulness exercise, or to practice informally. Just make sure to make it a daily habit.
10. **_Don't make excuses._** When you encounter distractions and start feeling frustrated, don't make excuses that mindfulness just isn't for you, or that you try another time. You're just enforcing negative thoughts again. Remember, mindfulness has been scientifically proven and anybody can learn it. Once you begin to feel the tranquility and peace it brings you, you will want to bring mindfulness into every aspect of your life.

When we cultivate mindfulness, we empower ourselves to stay grounded in the present and deal with problems confidently and calmly, rather than being controlled by negative memories and worries about the future.

Mindfulness is an integral part of your process of rewiring the mind and taking control of your life. If you have never practiced mindfulness techniques before, I won't lie to you; it won't be easy at first or even relaxing. But I can't urge you enough to stick to it because the rewards are immense. Over time, you will discover that mindfulness is a key part of your overall happiness and wellbeing.

Chapter 10 Practicing Mindfulness

When you overthink, you detach yourself from the present moment. You become blissfully unaware of where you are, and what you are doing, it's as if you are on auto-pilot, but the thing is that you are only going around in circles. If you are a chronic overthinker, you need to find a way to snap yourself out of this vicious thought cycle before it sucks you in deeper, and this is where mindfulness can help.

Actually, mindfulness practice is not just for snapping you out of your overthinking habit, it can actually minimize the times you overthink, and maybe even eliminate this bad habit entirely.

What is Mindfulness?

If this is the first time you encountered the term "mindfulness", it is similar to meditation, but at the same time it is different as well. There are some concepts that are shared between the two practices, but they are not that many. Being mindful is being aware, but not judgmental, of what you are currently experiencing (including your thoughts and emotions) in the present moment. It being aware of yourself and your present moment. You might think that you are already naturally aware of yourself, but you will learn that it is actually a skill that you are still yet to develop.

Most people live their lives the way their thinking minds and egos dictate them. Some researchers call this unconscious perspective as the person's Default Mode Network, or DMN for short. Your DMN filters your present perceptions based on your past experiences, recurring habits, and any and all beliefs and/or opinions that you have developed in your life; the problem here is that it does not discern if the information it got is true or not. In order to be aware about the truth of the thoughts in your mind, you need to practice mindfulness.

People spend a majority of their time living as the voice that is inside their heads, and that voice is constantly analyzing and judging everything, and is always blabbering about useless stuff, and they often come with distracting mental images so they can hold onto their attention rather than let them take notice of what is really happening around them.

The truth is that everyone is conditioned to always be detached from the present. Do you think that you are better than most people? If you think so then you are most likely not. People who believe that they are not conditioned to act, think, and decide according to their habits and past experiences are the one who are more prone to overthinking and detaching from the present. These people are blissfully unaware of their conditioning, which leads to them living an "unconscious" life.

Mindfulness is a person's ability to be fully present in the moment; it is being aware of where you are and what you are currently doing, but also not being overly reactive or easily overwhelmed by the things that are going on around you. And although mindfulness is something that is naturally within every person, it becomes more effective when it is practiced every day.

When you make yourself aware to what you are experiencing by using your senses, or to your state of mind by analyzing your thoughts and feelings, you are being mindful. There are actually quite a number of medical researches that shows that with consistent mindfulness training, you are actually remolding the physical structure of your brain.

With this in mind (pardon the pun), the goal of mindfulness is to make yourself aware of the intricacies of your mental, emotional, and physical processes. It is basically you learning more about yourself.

What is Meditation?

When you meditate, you let your mind wander; there is no fixed destination, there are no finish lines to tell you when to stop, you just go where you want to go. Unbeknownst to many, meditating does not mean that your brain will be devoid of any and all thoughts, it does not completely eliminate distractions, it does not turn you into an empty vessel. Meditating is like you going to your special place where every second of every moment receives special treatment.

When you are meditating, you venture into the innermost

workings of your mind, you are more in touch with your senses (you notice the air blowing on your skin, you get a waft of the flowers on the mantle, etc.), your emotions (you love feeling this way, or you hate it, you crave for something, etc.), and with your thoughts (this is where you notice your irrational thoughts that trigger overthinking).

Mindfulness only asks that you suspend judgment and for once become curious about how your mind works; and you do so with kindness, both to yourself and to others.

What Mindfulness Is NOT

Before you start learning more about mindfulness practice, you need to get the records straight about it. Here are five things that people usually get wrong about mindfulness:

1. *Mindfulness will not "fix" you*

If you are suffering from any form of mental illness, be warned that mindfulness cannot cure you, nor does it claim to. Mindfulness can only help you deal with the symptoms, but it cannot fix the underlying ailment.

2. *Mindfulness is not about stopping your thoughts or clearing your mind*

When you practice mindfulness, you are not shutting down your brain. You are not emptying your mind of all thought. In fact, you are only actually acknowledging all of the unwanted thoughts in your mind so they can leave on their own.

When you finish meditating, your thoughts are still in your head, but they will not be bothering you as much, and most of them are on their way out.

3. Mindfulness does not belong to any religion or sect

Anyone can practice mindfulness. Christians, Muslims, even atheists can all practice mindfulness. No one religion claims to have exclusive rights to meditating, you can practice meditation regardless if you are religious or not. You can also include some aspects of your belief into your meditation; for instance, if you are a devout Catholic, you can use prayers to meditate, or if you are a Buddhist, you can use mantras to get into the right headspace.

4. Mindfulness does not help you escape from reality

Just like how it does not help empty your mind, mindfulness also does not let you escape from reality. What many people thought about meditation is actually false. For instance, you cannot escape the real world and escape to a "happy place" in your mind. The truth is that mindfulness actually makes you more aware of the things that are happening around you, which is the polar opposite. Escaping to a "happy place" is only a stop-gap solution, when you get out of your happy place your problems are still in the real world.

5. *Mindfulness is not a panacea*

Mindfulness is not, nor has it ever claimed to be a cure-all for anything that ails you. If you are suffering from any sort of medical condition, you should seek treatment from a medical doctor, do not rely on mindfulness to let you "think" your sickness away. Many have tried to "fix" themselves this way, and most, if not all, of them have failed miserably. Meditation is just like a maintenance medication of sorts, it aids in proper treatment, but it is not the main treatment.

Why You Need to Practice Mindfulness

You can practice mindfulness in every moment. You can either choose to meditate and perform body scans in a quiet room, or for instance, when your phone rings, you can pause and take a deep breath before answering it. To make you even more motivated to practice mindfulness, here are some of its benefits:

It Turns You into A Better Decision-maker

One of the main problems of making a habit out of DMN is that you think that you only have limited choices to make decisions. Rather than considering if something can be good (or bad), you just act on whatever things might come by default. The more you subject yourself to this habit of yours, the more ingrained in your mind it becomes, until such time comes when you do it without even thinking about your best interests. Even just two weeks of mindfulness practice can greatly reduce instances of wandering minds and it also helped people improve their focus. In addition, mindfulness empowers people to be more creative and clearer when making decisions, especially those concerning their finances.

Mindfulness also trains your mind to work more efficiently. Researchers compared the brains scans of mindfulness practitioners to a control group. The results showed that the mindfulness group had more executive control, in other words, they are better decision-makers. The practitioners also had better mental acuity according to tests done after they practice mindfulness.

It Provides You with A Place Where You Can Be Free from Conditioning

How many times have you watched the evening news and there always seem to be at least one news item that grinds your gears? It is quite unfortunate that most people go through life reactively. Mindfulness provides you with awareness and a space in your head that allows you to choose how to respond, rather than having a knee-jerk reaction to things. You get a chance to choose your reaction rather than letting your mind default to the kinds of reactions that society has ingrained into you.

It Allows You to Increase Your Emotional Intelligence

Have you ever been angry at someone and then later regretted lashing out on that person? How many times have you started crying and then immediately regretted it because you could not stop? Are you easily startled by even the smallest thing? Do you have a nasty habit of losing your temper? If you think that your emotions are starting to take over your life, you need to practice mindfulness.

Medical studies have shown that people who practice mindfulness have better control over their emotions compared to other people. In fact, the US Military conducted their own research on mindfulness and how it could help sufferers of PTSD. Their research yielded that mindfulness can actually help minimize stress, and even ease the effects of chronic stress.

Mindfulness practice also helps people deal with change much better, become less dependent on the opinions of others, and also become more resilient when it comes to facing unpleasant emotions. Practicing mindfulness creates a bit of space between you and your emotions so you will have more time to process them and react to them accordingly.

Mindfulness training not only makes you more mature emotionally, you also gain more empathy, compassion, and you also become more altruistic.

After even just eight weeks, you will feel more empathy with others, and you are also more able to take compassionate action.

It Helps Your Body Thrive

Lots of athletes from all over the world use mindfulness to improve their performance. University basketball players practice mindfulness to help them accept their negative thoughts so they will not get nervous during the game, surfers practice mindfulness so they can get a hold of their fears and ride those humongous waves.

Mindfulness can also increase the amount of physical activity that your body can endure. Most people distract themselves from their workouts, but it is actually better when you practice mindfulness while you are working out. For instance, if you are in a hurry to finish your weight training workout, you will only focus on doing the requisite number of repetitions, and not pay attention to your form. And when you are not careful about your lifting form, you are more prone to getting seriously injured. With mindfulness, not only are you careful about your weightlifting form, you will also feel more accomplished with every set that you complete.

It Helps You Become More Creative

Regardless if it is with writing, drawing, sculpting, and other arts, you can use mindfulness to increase your creativity.

Creativity arises from the DMN. In these periods of unfocused rest, you have the chance to have a different perspective, you can make new associations between ideas and strike upon them. For instance, if you are a sculptor, you do not immediately know what to carve out of a huge chunk of stone. You need to sit in front of that huge slab of stone, and visualize what you can make out of it. The only way to see the final sculpture clearly is to eliminate all distractions around you.

The greatest obstacle to your creativity is the distractions that are around you. When your mind is distracted, it cannot switch from the its task-positive mode back to the DMN, which leads you to getting stuck in a rut. To make things worse, these distractions come in many different forms, from your regular daily tasks, to the different ongoing stressors that you have to deal with (like relationship and money problems).

With mindfulness, you can say goodbye to all of your distractions, and say hello to an almost infinite source of inspiration.

It Helps Strengthen Existing Neural Connections and Build New Ones

Remember earlier when it was mentioned that mindfulness can actually reshape the human brain, it meant in terms of creating new neural connections.

Practicing mindfulness as often as you can will cause your

brain to build new neural pathways, and ultimately new neural networks, thus making it function more efficiently. This helps your brain by improving concentration and awareness.

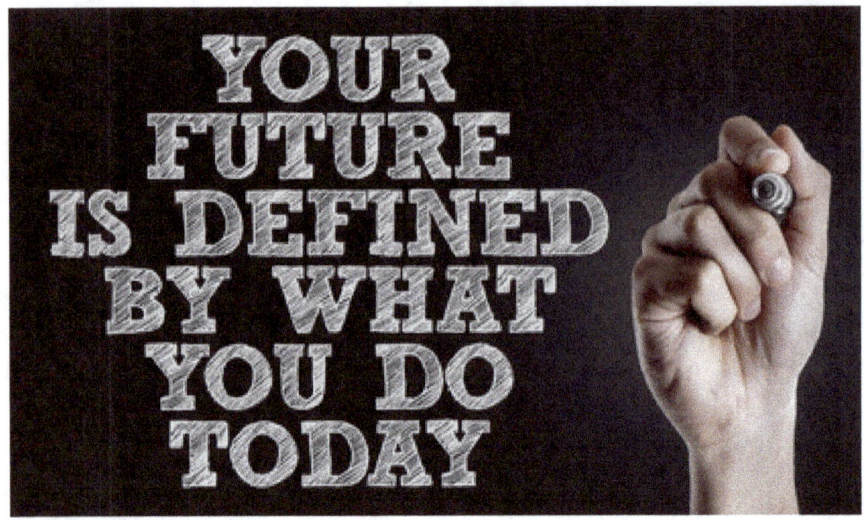

What Do You Need to Do to be More Mindful?

Practice mindfulness ad nauseam. There is no shortcut or magic pill that will help you become instantly more mindful. This book does not promise instant results, although you will receive tips that will make the process much easier, but it will still take you some time before you can become fully mindful. Being mindful means that you are training your mind to be aware of what it is thinking, rather than becoming what it is actually thinking.

This is where meditation can help you. There are many ways to meditate, the traditional method of sitting in a quiet place and observing your thoughts without being judgmental is the easiest way, and is also the best place to start for beginners. It might sound simple, but the problem is that most people are not living in the present, they are constantly worrying about things that are yet to happen, or happened already. Your thoughts are constantly running around uncontrolled in your brain. With mindfulness, you can put a bit of space around your thoughts so you can easily let go of comparisons, judgments, and control of them.

The Basics of Mindfulness-Based

Now, you will be learning how you can actually practice mindfulness. Here are some ways that you can help tune your mind into becoming more mindful every day:

Set aside time for practice. The great thing about mindfulness practice is that you do not need a fancy meditation cushion, or any other special equipment. However, you do need to set aside some time in your day for practicing mindfulness.

Observe the now. As mentioned earlier, mindfulness is not about silencing your thoughts, nor is it about attaining absolute inner peace. The ultimate goal of mindfulness is to train your mind to pay attention to the present moment, all without being judgmental of it; and this is easier said than done.

Let your judgments pass you by. Speaking of being judgmental, whenever you do notice that you are beginning to judge your views of the now, just take a mental note of your judgmental thoughts, and then let them drift past you.

Go back to observing the now. One cannot be mindful all the time, but one can return back to being mindful anytime. You cannot help it if your mind gets carried away sometime, especially when you are lost deep in your thoughts, but with mindfulness, you can drag yourself back into observing the now.

Be kind to your mind. Removing judgment is not just for your thoughts, you should also extend the same courtesy to your mind as well. Do not judge yourself if ever some irrational thoughts pop into your head, things like this happen all the time. The important thing is that you recognize when these things happen, and gently bring your mind back to the present.

Get a change of scenery. When you start to feel worried, get up and move to a new location. Not that many people are aware that their environment can also affect their moods. If you start feeling anxious while you are in a quiet room, go to where there is a bit more life. If you are getting overwhelmed by noise and too much energy, go somewhere quiet. The idea here is to disrupt your thoughts by giving it new sensations to process.

Do something to get your creative juices flowing.
Creativity has a different way of using your brain compared to how it is used by doing mundane tasks. Do not think that you are not creative, or that you do not have the talent for anything; everyone is creative, and that includes you of course. The problem is that you shut out your creative side because you feel that you are not good enough, or that it is just a waste of your time. Creativity is more than just the end-product, it is the entire process. Do not worry if you do not produce something that is beautiful in the broad sense, just create things that you can be proud of.

Get moving. One of the best things that you can do to fix your worried mind is to get a bit more physical. When you exercise your brain releases endorphins, these are brain chemicals that will make you feel happier, more relaxed, and less stressed.

Use your strengths. When you do something that you know you are good at, it is almost impossible not to feel good. It is never a bad thing to try something new, but if you feel as if you are starting to struggle and you are beginning to feel a bit overwhelmed, do something that you know you excel at. For instance, if you are a good baker, whip up a batch of your favorite muffins or cookies.

Are you great at gardening? Putter around in your garden for a bit, maybe even pick a couple of flowers so you have something refreshing on your work desk. These activities will help you snap out of your funk and get back to living in the now.

Distract yourself by doing something that uses brainpower. Distraction is one way to easily rid yourself of anxiety and worry. However, some types of distractions are better than others. For instance, for some people, binge-watching their favorite series on Netflix is a great way to deal with their anxious minds, but there are also some people who cannot shut their brain even if they are watching TV. If you are one of them, you can try other activities that require a bit more thinking and reasoning, like a Sudoku puzzle, a crossword puzzle, or trying your hand at a rather complicated craft that you saw online.

Make use of all your senses. An effective way to ground yourself back into the present is by using all of your senses to notice what is in front of you. Notice how many windows there are inside the room? Can you smell something cooking in the kitchen? How does the cushion on your chair feel? Can you hear that slight humming sound coming from the AC? Doing this engages your brain and distracts it from your worries, which then immediately grounds you back into the present.

Breathe deeply. The great thing about breathing exercises to deal with anxiety and worry is that you can do it anywhere you like. There are many breathing exercises that you can try, and all of them are readily available online.

However, all that you need to do is to slow down your breathing and focus on inhaling and exhaling. Count to five when you inhale and notice your chest rise, and then count to five as you exhale and notice your chest drop. Not only does focusing on your breath bring you back to the present, the increased amount of oxygen in your system also helps calm you down.

A Simple Mindfulness Meditation Practice for Beginners

If this is your first time to try meditation then you might feel a bit anxious and nervous that you might do it wrong and thus negate its effects; don't. There is absolutely no way that you can mess up with mindfulness meditation, you do not even need to follow the proceeding instructions to the letter, do with it as you want, the effects will still be relatively the same.

1. ***Sit in a comfortable position.*** It does not matter where you sit (on the floor, on a chair, on your couch, and others) as long as you are comfortable then that is fine. Just make sure that you are sitting on something that is stable and comfy.
2. ***Take notice of what your legs are doing.*** If you are sitting cross-legged on a cushion, notice how your legs intertwine and which parts are experiencing more pressure than others. If you are on a chair, notice how the

bottoms of your feet lie flat on the floor.

3. **Keep your back straight.** You should keep your back as straight as you can, however, do not stiffen up. Your backbone has a natural curvature, so let it rest in that position.

4. ***Take note of what your arms are doing.*** Position your arms in such a way that your upper arms are more or less parallel to your upper body, and place your palms on your legs anywhere you feel most comfortable.

5. ***Soften your gaze.*** Tilt your head a bit downward and let your gaze follow. You do not have to close your eyes. You can just let your eyes fall where they want. If there are objects in front of your eyes, just let them be there, do not focus on them.

6. **Feel your breath.** Point your thoughts toward your breath. Take notice of the air moving into your nose and going out of your mouth, and the rising of your chest with every breath.

7. **Keep an eye out for the times when your attention sways away from your breath.** There will always be times when your mind will wander away from your breath, do not worry when this happens. You do not have to block or avoid your thoughts, just gently coax your mind back to focusing on your breath.

8. ***Take it easy on your mind.*** You might find your mind constantly wander while you are meditating, do not be too hard on yourself, this kind of thing happens all the time. Instead of fighting your thoughts, you should practice just observing them, do not judge them and do not react to them, and just sit there and pay attention to your breath.
9. ***When you are ready, lift your gaze.*** When you are ready (do not worry because you will know when you are ready), take a moment to notice any sounds around you. Notice all of the sensations that your body is feeling, and then take notice of your thoughts and your emotions.

You just finished your first mindfulness meditation, that was not so bad now wasn't it? Again, you do not have to follow the instructions to the last detail, just as long as you feel the way you should then you did just fine.

Conclusion

Sometimes it can be hard to distinguish between destructive thoughts, overthinking and anxiety. People have likened these issues to the 'chicken and the egg' situation in that it is difficult to determine what came first; does one have anxiety because they started to overthink things or did, they start to overthink things because they suffered with anxiety?

Many people suffer with overthinking on a daily basis without realizing that they are doing it, many people will make hundreds of 'to do' lists telling themselves that they are organized and being prepared. There is nothing wrong with this yet if you are the type to make lists for everything, ask yourself "are you following them?" Are you crossing things off your list and achieving them or are you simply making a list, which you then worry about doing and shortly afterwards make another list without every actually completing anything?

Overthinking can be debilitating, once it starts to hold you back and prevents you from doing the things you want to do then it becomes a problem. However, once you realize you have an issue then you can do something about it.

Our brains are amazing yet being trapped inside our own can horrendous, our own personal hell. Nobody is more negative on ourselves than we are. Start using your overthinking in a positive way; instead of creating problems, try solving them. You can do this by making your to do list but also adding ways to do each item. For example, instead of just writing 'tidy the house' break it into bite size pieces such as 'clean the bath', 'sort out old clothes for the charity' and so on. If it is a work related problem such as meeting a deadline then break it into small chunks, for example, if you are writing a report, put a date to complete each section such as on Monday I'm going to write the introduction, on Tuesday I'm going to gather statistics, and so on.

Another great tool is self-reflection. Many people mix this up with overthinking but self-reflection is healthy when it involves learning about yourself and takes into account both your strengths as well as your weaknesses. Self-reflection allows you to look at a situation in a different way in order to see things from another perspective and used correctly is a great learning tool. Overthinking on the other hand doesn't help you gain new insight or perspective because you are too busy dwelling on the negatives and often worrying about things out of your control.

If you are prone to overthinking then sometimes you just need to halt the mental chatter by switching your thoughts to something else. Mental strength exercises are good for this and there are many resources out there to instruct you in how to do this.

Switching tasks and carrying out a physical activity can be a great way to clear our minds. Some people find relaxing physical activity such as Yoga can empty their thoughts whilst others like something more strenuous like running. Sometimes even just getting up for a short walk can help so if you are stuck in a cycle of negativity and destructive thoughts try getting up and moving about.

The ideas in this book should hopefully have given you something else to focus on but there isn't a 'one size fits all' solution. What works for some doesn't work for everyone and sometimes what works for you one day doesn't work on another day. It really is about trial and error and sticking with it over time.

If you find your overthinking and anxiety is getting the better of you then turn to somebody. We can't always go it alone no matter how independent we want to be. If you have a friend or family member you feel comfortable with then go to them or if you would feel better speaking to somebody completely impartial then you may prefer to see a doctor or a mental health specialist who can help. Whatever you choose, remember there is no shame asking for help and nobody is judging you except you.

www.ingramcontent.com/pod-product-compliance
Lightning Source LLC
Chambersburg PA
CBHW070914080526
44589CB00013B/1285